India—What Can It Teach Us?

India—What Can It Teach Us? is a series of lectures, delivered by F. Max Muller in 1882 at Cambridge, intended for the candidates for the Indian Civil Services. He projected his idea of India and of Hindu religion in its most ancient form based on a study of Sanskrit literatures, to the religious life of the Hindus of his time.

Max Müller vehemently denounced the habitual denigration of the Indian character by those Englishmen who lived in India or had first-hand experience of the country. He thus, set himself not only to defend Indians but also to show in what way the Indian character and outlook could be a complement to those of the European.

In his second and third lectures Max Müller grappled with prejudice that consisted in looking upon stay in India as a kind of moral exile and in regarding the Hindus as an inferior race. On the basis of facts and testimonies from Hindu scriptures foreign accounts and Colonel Sleeman's observations, he clearly showed the truthful character of the Hindus.

Lecture four seeks to clear doubts on the basis of evidences in the original texts regarding the historical importance of Vedic literature.

Lecture five is concerned with the study of religion and mythology revealed in Vedic literature, and Lecture six discusses, in detail, the Vedic deities. Lecture seven is devoted to answering questions as to how the Vedic literature could have been composed and preserved, if writing was unknown to India before 500 BC.

F. Max Müller (1823–1900), a "Scholar extraordinary" was regarded as one of the distinguished figures of Oxford where for many years he was Professor of Comparative Philology. He did more than anyone to promote the understanding of Indian thought through his teachings and works, like the edition of the *Rgveda* and through the Sacred Books of the East (SBE, a series of religious books). He roused interest and enthusiasm in Vedic literature, Sanskrit, philology, mythology in a way which made them components in the general culture of his times.

Prof. K.A. Nilakanta Sastri (1892–1975) was one of the foremost historians of India, whose numerous writings on south India have been acclaimed for their scholarship in India and abroad.

India–What Can It Teach Us?

F. Max Müller

Indian edition by

K.A. Nilakanta Sastri

Munshiram Manoharlal
Publishers Pvt. Ltd.

ISBN 978-81-215-0394-5
Reprinted 1900, 1938, 1991, 2005, **2015**
First published 1880

PRINTED IN INDIA
Published by Vikram Jain *for*
Munshiram Manoharlal Publishers Pvt. Ltd.
PO Box 5715, 54 Rani Jhansi Road, New Delhi 110 055, INDIA

www.mrmlbooks.com

Contents

DEDICATED TO

E.B. COWELL, M.A., LL.D

PROFESSOR OF SANSKRIT AND FELLOW OF CORPUS CHRISTI COLLEGE
IN THE UNIVERSITY OF CAMBRIDGE

Dedication

My Dear Cowell,

As these Lectures would never have been written or delivered but for your hearty encouragement, I hope you will now allow me to dedicate them to you, not only as a token of my sincere admiration of your great achievements as an Oriental scholar, but also as a memorial of our friendship, now more than thirty years old, a friendship which has grown from year to year, has weathered many a storm, and will last, I trust, for what to both of us may remain of our short passage from shore to shore.

I must add, however, that in dedicating these Lectures to you, I do not wish to throw upon you any responsibility for the views which I have put forward in them. I know that you do not agree with some of my views on the ancient religion and literature of India, and I am well aware that with regard to the recent date which I have assigned to the whole of what is commonly called the Classical Sanskrit Literature, I stand almost alone. No, if friendship can claim any voice in the courts of science and literature, let me assure you that I shall consider your outspoken criticism of my Lectures as the very best proof of your true and honest friendship. I have through life considered it the greatest honour if real scholars, I mean men not only of learning, but of judgment and character, have considered my writings worthy of a severe and searching criticism, and I have cared far more for the production of single new fact, though it spoke against me, than for any amount of empty praise or empty abuse. Sincere devotion to his studies and an unswerving love of truth ought to furnish the true scholar with an armour impermeable to flattery or abuse, but with a vizor that shuts out no ray of light, from whatever quarter it may come. More light, more truth, more facts, more combination of facts, these are his quest. And if in that quest he fails, as many have failed before him, he knows that in the search for truth failures are sometimes the condition of success, and the true conquerors often those whom the world calls the vanquished.

You know better than anybody else the present state of Sanskrit scholarship. You know that at present and for some time to come Sanskrit scholarship means discovery and conquest. Every one of your own works marks a real advance, and a permanent occupation of new ground. But you know also how small a strip has as yet been explored of the vast continent of Sanskrit literature, and how much still remains *terra incognita*. No doubt this exploring work is troublesome, and often disappointing, but young students must learn the truth of a remark lately made by a distinguished member of the Indian Civil Service, whose death we all deplore, Dr. Burnell, 'that no trouble is thrown away which saves trouble to others.' We want men who will work hard, even at the risk of seeing their labours unrequited, we want strong and bold men who are not afraid of storms and shipwrecks. The worst sailors are not those who suffer shipwreck, but those who only dabble in puddles and are afraid of wetting their feet.

It is easy now to criticise the labours of Sir William Jones, Thomas Colebrooke, and Horace Hayman Wilson, but what would have become of Sanskrit scholarship, if they had not rushed in where even now so many fear to tread? and what will become of Sanskrit scholarship, if their conquests are for ever to mark the limits of our knowledge? You know best that there is more to be discovered in Sanskrit literature than Nalas and Sakuntalas, and surely the young men who every year go out to India are not deficient in the spirit of enterprise, or even of adventure? Why then should it be said that the race of bold explorers, who once rendered the name of the Indian Civil Service illustrious over the whole world, has well-nigh become extinct, and that England, which offers the strongest incentives and the most brilliant opportunities for the study of the ancient language, literature, and history of India, is no longer in the van of Sanskrit scholarship?

If some of the young candidates for the Indian Civil Service who listened to my Lectures, made up their minds that such a reproach shall be wiped out, if a few of them at least determined to follow in the footsteps of Sir William Jones, and to show to the world that Englishmen who have been able to achieve by pluck, by perseverance, and by real political genius the material conquest of India, do not mean to leave the laurels of its intellectual conquest entirely to other countries, then I shall indeed rejoice, and feel that I have paid back, in however small a degree, the large debt of gratitude which I owe to my adopted country and to some of its greatest statesmen, who have given me the opportunity which I could find nowhere else of realising the dreams of my life,—the publication of the text and commentary of the *Rigveda*, the most ancient book of Sanskrit, aye of Aryan literature, and now the edition of the translations of the *Sacred Books of the East*.

I have left my Lectures very much as I delivered them at Cambridge. I am fond of the form of Lectures, because it seems to me the most natural form which in our age didactic composition ought to take. As in ancient Greece the dialogue reflected most truly the intellectual life of the people, and as in the Middle Ages learned literature naturally assumed with the recluse in his monastic cell the form of a long monologue, so with us the lecture places the writer most readily in that position in which he is accustomed to deal with his fellow-men, and to communicate his knowledge to others. It has no doubt certain disadvantages. In a lecture which is meant to be didactic we have, for the sake of completeness, to say and to repeat certain things which must be familiar to some of our readers, while we are also forced to leave out information which, even in its imperfect form, we should probably not hesitate to submit to our fellow-students, but which we feel we have not yet sufficiently, mastered and matured to enable us to place it clearly and simply before a larger public.

But the advantages outweigh the disadvantages. A lecture, by keeping a critical audience constantly before our eyes, forces us to condense our subject, to discriminate between what is important and what is not, and often to deny ourselves the pleasure of displaying what may have cost us the greatest labour, but is of little consequence to other scholars. In lecturing we are constantly reminded of what students are so apt to forget, that their knowledge is meant not for themselves only, but for others, and that to know well means to be able to teach well. I confess I can never write unless I think of somebody for whom I write, and I should never wish for a better audience to have before my mind than the learned, brilliant, and kind-hearted assembly by which I was greeted in your university.

Still I must confess that I did not succeed in bringing all I wished to say, and more particularly the evidence on which some of my statements rested, up to the higher level of a lecture, and I have therefore added a number of notes[1] containing the less organised matter which resisted as yet that treatment which is necessary before our studies can realise their highest purpose, that of feeding, invigorating, and inspiriting the minds of others.

Yours affectionately,
F. MAX MÜLLER

Oxford
December 16, 1882

[1]These notes have been omitted in this edition.

The Life and Works of Max Muller

FRIEDRICH MAX MÜLLER was born at Dessau on the 6th December 1823. He was the only son of the distinguished poet Wilhelm Müller who died in 1827. Max Müller showed a talent for music early in life, but he was dissuaded by Mendelssohn from adopting music as his profession. At school he decided to devote himself to the classical languages. He entered the University of Leipzig in 1841, began to learn Sanskrit, and published a translation of the *Hitopadesa* in 1844, after graduating Ph.D. on September 1, 1843. He then went to Berlin and attended the lectures of Bopp and Schelling, and thus began that attachment to philology and philosophy which lasted all his life. In 1845 he migrated to Paris and came under the influence of Eugene Burnouf, at whose suggestion he started collecting materials for the *editio princeps* of the *Rigveda*. While engaged on this work, he had to struggle for his livelihood and to maintain himself by copying manuscripts and assisting scholars in other ways. He went to England in 1846, and the Board of Directors of the East India Company commissioned him to bring out at their expense a complete edition of the *Rigveda* with Sayana's commentary. He went back to Paris in 1848 to collate manuscripts, but, on the outbreak of the Revolution, fearing for the safety of his manuscripts, he returned quickly to London.

Soon after, the printing of the first volume began at the Oxford University Press, and he found it necessary to go and settle in Oxford, which became his home for the rest of his life. He became Deputy Taylorian Professor of Modern European Languages in 1850 and succeeded to the professorship in 1854. In 1859 he published his *History of Ancient Sanskrit Literature*, a work containing much valuable and important research in literary chronology, based on a knowledge of many works then available only in manuscript.

H.H. Wilson, Professor of Sanskrit at Oxford, died in 1860 (May). Max Müller had strong claims to succeed him on account of his ability and published work; but he was a foreigner and his broad views on theological questions were well known; and the election to the post was in the hands of Convocation. The country clergy decided the election against Max Müller, who was, no doubt, bitterly disappointed with the result.

Max Müller's great capacities and industry were now forced to find empolyment along other channels. His lectures on the *Science of Language* delivered in 1861 and 1863 at the Royal Institution made him a recognised authority in England and gave evidence of his marvellous powers of lucid exposition and of presenting dry subjects in a fascinating manner. The same subject was continued in his *Science of Thought* (1887). He retired from the Taylorian professorship in 1868 and became the first Professor of Comparative Philology from that year. He wrote extensively on subjects of Comparative Mythology; but though his work on this subject has not stood the test of time, it gave a great stimulus to its study. In the field of Comparative Religion again, he was a pioneer, being the first Hibbert Lecturer. In 1878 he lectured under this foundation on the *Origin and Growth of Religion,* and was again Hibbert Lecturer during the years 1888 to 1892. When he gave up active service as Professor of Comparative Philology in 1875, he embarked on what was perhaps the greatest and most important undertaking of his life—the planning and editing of the *Sacred Books of the East*..., he himself contributing three complete volumes and parts of two others out of a total of fifty-one.

He kept up his pursuit of Sanskrit studies. The *Rigveda* was finished in 1873, and a second revised edition brought out in 1892. He initiated the Aryan series in the Anecdota Oxoniensia with four publication of his own, and assisted in planning the next three which appeared before 1900. His Cambridge lecture (1882) on *India—What Can it Teach Us?* came out as a book in 1883. He helped scholars who went to Oxford for the study of Sanskrit with suggestions for suitable lines of work.

Among his other works are: *Chips from a German Workshop* (four volumes), being a collection of his contributions to the English journals; *Auld Lang Syne* (vol. I, 1898; II, 1899), a book of reminiscences; *Deutsche Liebe* (1857), a German romance, translated into several other European languages.

Though a busy scholar and voluminous writer, Max Müller was 'quite a man of the world.' He was acquainted with most of the leading men of Europe in his day, including several crowned heads. 'On account of his social qualities Max Müller was much in request as president of societies and congresses.' Degrees, titles, and honours poured on him from all the European countries.

He died at Oxford on October 28, 1900.[1]

[1]For further details see the article of A.A. Macdonell in the *Dictionary of National Biography* on which this sketch is based.

LECTURE I

What Can India Teach Us?

WHEN I received from the Board of Historical Studies at Cambridge the invitation to deliver a course of lectures, specially intended for the candidates for the Indian Civil Service, I hesitated for some time, feeling extremely doubtful whether in a few public discourses I could say anything that would be of real use to them in passing their examinations. To enable young men to pass their examinations seems now to have become the chief, if not the only object of the Universities; and to no class of students is it of greater importance to pass their examinations, and to pass them well, than to the candidates for the Indian Civil Service.

But although I was afraid that attendance on a few public lectures, such as I could give, would hardly benefit a candidate who was not already fully prepared to pass through the fiery ordeal of the three London examinations, I could not on the other hand shut my eyes completely to the fact that, after all, Universities were not meant entirely, or even chiefly, as stepping-stones to an examination, but that there is something else which Universities can teach and ought to teach—nay, which I feel quite sure they were originally meant to teach—something that may not have a marketable value before a Board of Examiners, but which has a permanent value for the whole of our life,—and that is a real interest in our work, and more than that, a love of our work, and more than that, a true joy and happiness in our work. If a University can teach that, if it can engraft that one small living germ in the minds of the young men who come here to study and to prepare themselves for the battle of life, and, for what is still more difficult to encounter, the daily dull drudgery of life, then, I feel convinced, a University has done more, and conferred a more lasting benefit on its pupils than by helping them to pass the most difficult examinations, and to take the highest place among Senior Wranglers or First-Class men.

Unfortunately that kind of work which is now required for passing one examination after another, that process of cramming and crowding, which has of late been brought to the highest pitch of perfection, has often the very opposite effect, and instead of exciting an appetite for work, it is apt to produce an indifference, if not a kind of intellectual nausea, that may last for life.

And nowhere is this so much to be feared as in the case of candidates for the Indian Civil Service. After they have passed their first examination for admission to the Indian Civil Service, and given proof that they have received the benefits of a liberal education, and acquired that general information in classics, history, and mathematics, which is provided at our Public Schools, and forms no doubt the best and surest foundation for all more special and professional studies in later life, they suddenly find themselves torn away from their old studies and their old friends, and compelled to take up new subjects which to many of them seem strange, outlandish, if not repulsive. Strange alphabets, strange languages, strange names, strange literatures and laws have to be faced, 'to be got up' as it is called, not from choice, but from dire necessity. The whole course of study during two years is determined for them, the subjects fixed, the books prescribed, the examinations regulated, and there is no time to look either right or left, if a candidate wishes to make sure of taking each successive fence in good style, and without an accident.

I know quite well that this cannot be helped. I am not speaking against the system of examinations in general, if only they are intelligently conducted; nay, as an old examiner myself, I feel bound to say that the amount of knowledge produced ready-made at these examinations is to my mind perfectly astounding. But while the answers are there on paper, strings of dates, lists of royal names and battles, irregular verbs, statistical figures and whatever else you like, how seldom do we find that the heart of the candidates is in the work which they have to do. The results produced are certainly most ample and voluminous, but they rarely contain a spark of original thought, or even a clever mistake. It is work done from necessity, or, let us be just, from a sense of duty, but it is seldom, or hardly ever, a labour of love.

Now why should that be? Why should a study of Greek and Latin,—of the poetry, the philosophy, the laws and the art of Greece and Italy,—seem congenial to us, why should it excite even a certain enthusiasm, and command general respect, while a study of Sanskrit, and of the ancient poetry, the philosophy, the laws, and the art of India is looked upon, in the best case, as curious, but is considered by most people as useless, tedious, if not absurd.

And, strange to say, this feeling exists in England more than in any other country. In France, Germany, and Italy, even in Denmark, Sweden, and Russia, there is a vague charm connected with the name of India. One of the most beautiful poems in the German language is the *Weisheit des Brahmanen*, the 'Wisdom of the Brahman,' by Rückert, to my mind more rich in thought and more perfect in form than even Goethe's *West-ostlicher Divan.* A scholar who studies Sanskrit in Germany is supposed to be initiated in the deep and dark mysteries of ancient wisdom, and a man who has travelled in India, even if he has only discovered Calcutta, or Bombay, or Madras, is listened to like another Marco Polo. In England a student of Sanskrit is generally considered a bore, and an old Indian Civil servant, if he begins to describe the marvels of Elephanta or the Towers of Silence, runs the risk of producing a count-out.

There are indeed a few Oriental scholars whose works are read, and who have acquired a certain celebrity in England, because they were really men of uncommon genius, and would have ranked among the great glories of the country, but for the misfortune that their energies were devoted to Indian literature—I mean Sir William Jones, 'one of the most enlightened of the sons of men,' as Dr. Johnson called him, and Thomas Colebrooke. But the names of others who have done good work in their day also, men such as Ballantyne. Buchanan, Carey, Crawfurd, Davis, Elliot, Ellis, Houghton, Leyden, Mackenzie, Marsden, Muir, Prinsep, Rennell, Turnour, Upham, Wallich, Warren, Wilkins, Wilson, and many others, are hardly known beyond the small circle of Oriental scholars, and their works are looked for in vain in libraries which profess to represent with a certain completeness the principal branches of scholarship and science in England.

How many times when I advised young men, candidates for the Indian Civil Service, to devote themselves before all things to a study of Sanskrit, have I been told, 'What is the use of our studying Sanskrit? There are translations of the *Sakuntala, Manu.*, and the *Hitopadesa,* and what else is there in that literature that is worth reading? Kalidasa may be very pretty, and the Laws of Manu are very curious, and the fables of the *Hitopadesa* are very quaint; but you would not compare Sanskrit literature with Greek, or recommend us to waste our time in copying and editing Sanskrit texts which either teach us nothing that we do not know already, or teach us something which we do not care to know?'

This seems to me a most unhappy misconception, and it will be the chief object of my lectures to try to remove it, or at all events to modify it, as much as possible. I shall not attempt to prove that Sanskrit literature is as good as Greek literature. Why should we always compare? A study of Greek literature has its own purpose, and a study of Sanskrit literature has its own purpose; but what I feel convinced of, and hope to convince you of, is that Sanskrit literature, if studied only in a right spirit, is full of human interests, full of lessons which even Greek could never teach us, a subject worthy to occupy the leisure, and more than the leisure, of every Indian Civil servant; and certainly the best means of making any young man who has to spend five-and-twenty years of his life in India, feel at home among the Indians, as a fellow-worker among fellow-workers, and not as an alien among aliens. There will be abundance of useful and most interesting work for him to do, if only he cares to do it, work such as he would look for in vain, whether in Italy or in Greece, or even among the pyramids of Egypt or the palaces of Babylon.

You will now understand why I have chosen as the title of my lectures, '*What can India teach us*?' True, there are many things, which India has to learn from us; but there are other things, and, in one sense, very important things, which we too may learn from India.

If I were to look over the whole world to find out the country most richly endowed with all the wealth, power, and beauty that nature can bestow—in some parts a very paradise on earth—I should point to India. If I were asked under what sky the human mind has most fully developed some of its choicest gifts, has most deeply pondered on the greatest problems of life, and has found solutions of some of them which well deserve the attention even of those who have studied Plato and Kant—I should point to India. And if I were to ask myself from what literature we, here in Europe, we who have been nurtured almost exclusively on the thoughts of Greeks and Romans, and of one Semitic race, the Jewish, may draw that corrective which is most wanted in order to make our inner life more perfect, more comprehensive, more universal, in fact more truly human, a life, not for this life only, but a transfigured and eternal life—again I should point to India.

I know you will be surprised to hear me say this, I know that more particularly those who have spent many years of active life in Calcutta, or Bombay, or Madras, will be horror-struck at the idea that the humanity they meet with there, whether in the bazaars or in the courts of justice, or in so-called native society, should be able to teach *us* any lessons.

Let me therefore explain at once to my friends who may have lived in India for years, as civil servants, or officers, or missionaries, or merchants, and who ought to know a great deal more of that country than one who has never set foot on the soil of Aryavarta, that we are speaking of two very different Indias. I am thinking chiefly of India, such as it was a thousand, two thousand, it may be three thousand years ago; they think of the India of today. And again, when thinking of the India of today, they remember chiefly the India of Calcutta, Bombay, or Madras, the India of the towns. I look to the India of the village communities, the true India of the Indians.

What I wish to show to you, I mean more especially the candidates for the Indian Civil Service, is that this India of a thousand, or two thousand, or three thousand years ago, aye the India of today also, if only you know where to look for it, is full of problems the solution of which concerns all of us, even us in this Europe of the nineteenth century.

If you have acquired any special tastes here in England, you will find plenty to satisfy them in India; and whoever has learnt to take an interest in any of the great problems that occupy the best thinkers and workers at home, need certainly not be afraid of India proving to him an intellectual exile.

If you care for geology, there is work for you from the Himalayas to Ceylon.

If you are fond of botany, there is a flora rich enough for many Hookers.

If you are a zoologist, think of Haeckel, who is just now rushing through Indian forests and dredging in Indian seas, and to whom his stay in India is like the realisation of the brightest dream of his life.

If you are interested in ethnology, why India is like a living ethnological museum.

If you are fond of archaeology, if you have ever assisted at the opening of a barrow in England, and know the delight of finding a fibula, or a knife, or a flint in a heap of rubbish, read only General Cunningham's *Annual Reports of the Archaeological Survey of India*, and you will be impatient for the time when you can take your spade and bring to light the ancient Viharas or Colleges built by the Buddhist monarchs of India.

If ever you amused yourselves with collecting coins, why the soil of India teems with coins, Persian, Carian, Thracian, Parthian, Greek, Macedonian, Scythian, Roman, and Mohammedan. When Warren Hastings was Governor-General, an earthen pot was found on the bank of a river in the province of Benares, containing 172 gold Darics. Warren Hastings considered himself as making the most munificent present to his masters that he might ever have it in his power to send them, by presenting those ancient coins to the Court of Directors. The story is that they were sent to the melting-pot. At all events they had disappeared when Warren Hastings returned to England. It rests with you to prevent the revival of such Vandalism.

The study of Mythology has assumed an entirely new character, chiefly owing to the light that has been thrown on it by the ancient Vedic Mythology of India. But though the foundation of a true Science of Mythology has been laid, all the detail has still to be worked out, and could be worked out nowhere better than in India.

Even the study of fables owes its new life to India, from whence the various migrations of fables have been traced at various times and through various channels from East to West. Buddhism is now known to have been the principal source of our legends and parables. But here too, many problems still wait for their solution. Think, for instance, of the allusion to the fable of the donkey in the lion's skin, which occurs in Plato's *Cratylus.* Was that borrowed from the East? Or take the fable of the weasel changed by Aphrodite into a woman, who, when she saw a mouse, could not refrain from making a spring at it. This, too, is very like a Sanskrit fable, but how then could it have been brought into Greece early enough to appear in one of the comedies of Strattis, about 400 BC ? Here, too, there is still plenty of work to do.

We may go back even further into antiquity, and still find strange coincidences between the legends of India and the legends of the West, without as yet being able to say how they travelled, whether from East to West, or from West to East. That at the time of Solomon, there was a channel of communication open between India and Syria and Palestine is established beyond doubt, I believe, by certain Sanskrit words which occur in the *Bible* as names of articles of export from Ophir, articles such as ivory, apes, peacocks, and sandalwood, which taken together, could not have been exported from any country but India. Nor is there any reason to suppose that the commercial intercourse between India, the Persian Gulf, the Red Sea and the Mediterranean was ever completely interrupted, even at the time when the Book of Kings is supposed to have been written.

Now you remember the judgement of Solomon, which has always been admired as a proof of great legal wisdom among the Jews. I must confess that, not having a legal mind, I never could suppress a certain shudder when reading the decision of Solomon: 'Divide the living child in two, and give half to the one, and half to the other.'

Let me now tell you the same story as it is told by the Buddhists, whose sacred Canon is full of such legends and parables. In the *Kanjur*, which is the Tibetan translation of the Buddhist *Tripitaka*, we read of two women who claimed each to be the mother of the same child. The king, after listening to their quarrels for a long time, gave it up as hopeless to settle who was the real mother. Upon this Visakha stepped forward and said: 'What is the use of examining and cross-examining these women. Let them take the boy and settle it among themselves.' Thereupon both women fell on the child, and when the fight became violent, the child was hurt and began to cry. Then one of them let him go, because she could not bear to hear the child cry.

That settled the question. The king gave the child to the true mother, and had the other beaten with a rod.

This seems to me, if not the more primitive, yet the more natural form of the story—showing a deeper knowledge of human nature, and more wisdom than even the wisdom of Solomon.

Many of you may have studied not only languages, but also the Science of Language, and is there any country in which some of the most important problems of that science, say only the growth and decay of dialects, or the possible mixture of languages, with regard not only to words, but to grammatical elements also, can be studied to greater advantage than among the Aryan, the Dravidian and the Munda inhabitants of India, when brought in contact with their various invaders and conquerors, the Greeks, the Yue-tchi, the Arabs, the Persians, the Moguls, and lastly the English.

Again, if you are a student of Jurisprudence, there is a history of law to be explored in India, very different from what is known of the history of law in Greece, in Rome, and in Germany, yet both by its contrasts and by its similarities full of suggestions to the student of Comparative Jurisprudence. New materials are being discovered every year, as, for instance, the so-called Dharma or Samayacharika Sutras, which have supplied the materials for the later metrical law-books, such as the famous Laws of Manu. What was once called 'The Code of Laws of Manu,' and confidently referred to 1,200, or at least 500 BC, is now hesitatingly referred to perhaps the fourth century AD, and called neither a Code, nor a Code of Laws, least of all, the Code of Laws of Manu.

If you have learnt to appreciate the value of recent researches into the antecedents of all law, namely the foundation and growth of the simplest political communities—and nowhere could you have had better opportunities for it than here at Cambridge—you will find a field of observation opened before you in the still existing village estates in India that will amply repay careful research.

And take that which, after all, whether we confess or deny it, we care for more in this life than for anything else—nay, which is often far more cared for by those who deny than by those who confess—take that which supports, pervades, and directs all our acts and thoughts and hopes—without which there can be neither village community nor empire, neither custom nor law, neither right nor wrong—take that which, next to language, has most firmly fixed the specific and permanent barrier between man and beast—which alone has made life possible and bearable, and which, as it is the deepest, though often hidden spring of individual life, is also the foundation of all national life,—the history of all histories, and yet the mystery of all mysteries—take religion, and where can you study its true origin, its natural growth, and its inevitable decay better than in India, the home of Brahmanism, the birthplace of Buddhism, and the refuge of Zoroastrianism, even now the mother of new superstitions—and why not, in the future, the regenerate child of the purest faith, if only purified from the dust of nineteen centuries?

You will find yourselves everywhere in India between an immense past and an immense future, with opportunities such as the old world could but seldom, if ever, offer you. Take any of the burning questions of the day—popular education, higher education, parliamentary representation, codification of laws, finance, emigration, poor-law, and whether you have anything to teach and to try, or anything to observe and to learn, India will supply you with a laboratory such as exists nowhere else. That very Sanskrit, the study of which may at first seem so tedious to you and so useless, if only you will carry it on, as you may carry it on here at Cambridge better than anywhere else, will open before you large layers of literature, as yet almost unknown and unexplored, and allow you an insight into strata of thought deeper than any you have known before, and rich in lessons that appeal to the deepest sympathies of the human heart.

Depend upon it, if only you can make leisure, you will find plenty of work in India for your leisure hours.

India is not, as you may imagine, a distant, strange, or, at the very utmost, a curious country. India for the future belongs to Europe, it has its place in the Indo-European world, it has its place in our own history, and in what is the very life of history, the history of the human mind.

You know how some of the best talent and the noblest genius of our age has been devoted to the study of the development of the outward or material world, the growth of the earth, the first appearance of living cells, their combination and differentiation, leading up to the beginning of organic life, and its steady progress from the lowest to the highest stages. Is there not an inward and intellectual world also which has to be studied in its historical development, from the first appearance of predicative and demonstrative roots, their combination and differentiation, leading up to the beginning of rational thought in its steady progress from the lowest to the highest stages? And in that study of the history of the human mind, in that study of ourselves, of our true selves, India occupies a place second to no other country. Whatever sphere of the human mind you may select for your special study, whether it be language, or religion, or mythology, or philosophy, whether it be laws or customs, primitive art or primitive science, everywhere, you have to go to India, whether you like it or not, because some of the most valuable and most instructive materials in the history of man are treasured up in India, and in India only.

And while thus trying to explain to those whose lot will soon be cast in India the true position which that wonderful country holds or ought to hold in universal history, I may perhaps be able at the same time to appeal to the sympathies of other members of this University, by showing them how imperfect our knowledge of universal history, our insight into the development of the human intellect, must always remain, if we narrow our horizon to the history of Greeks and Romans, Saxons and Celts, with a dim background of Palestine, Egypt, and Babylon, and leave out of sight our nearest intellectual relatives, the Aryas of India, the framers of the most wonderful language, the Sanskrit, the fellow-workers in the construction of our fundamental concepts, the fathers of the most natural of natural religions, the makers of the most transparent of mythologies, the inventors of the most subtle philosophy, and the givers of the most elaborate laws.

There are many things which we think essential in a liberal education, whole chapters of history which we teach in our schools and Universities, that cannot for one moment compare with the chapter relating to India, if only properly understood and freely interpreted.

In our time, when the study of history threatens to become almost an impossibility—such is the mass of details which historians collect in archives and pour out before us in monographs—it seems to me more than ever the duty of the true historian to find out the real proportion of things, to arrange his materials according to the strictest rules of artistic perspective, and to keep completely out of sight all that may be rightly ignored by us in our own passage across the historical stage of the world. It is this power of discovering what is really important that distinguished the true historian from the mere chronicler, in whose eyes everything is important, particularly if he has discovered it himself. I think it was Frederick the great who, when sighing for a true historian of his reign, complained bitterly that those who wrote the history of Prussia never forgot to describe the buttons on his uniform. And it is probably of such historical works that Carlyle was thinking when he said that he had waded through them all, but that nothing should ever induce him to hand even their names and titles down to posterity. And yet how much is there even in Carlyle's histories that might safely be consigned to oblivion!

Why do we want to know history? Why does history form a recognised part of our liberal education? Simply because all of us, and every one of us, ought to know how we have come to be what we are, so that each generation need not start again from the same point, and toil over the same ground, but, profiting by the experience of those who came before, may advance towards higher points and nobler aims. As a child when growing up, might ask his father or grandfather, *who* had built the house they lived in, or who had cleared the field that yielded them their food, we ask the historian whence we came, and how we came into possession of what we call our own. History may tell us afterwards many useful and amusing things, gossip, such as a child might like to hear from his mother or grandmother; but what history has to teach us before all and everything, is our own antecedents, our own ancestors, our own descent.

Now our principal intellectual ancestors are, no doubt, the Jews, the Greeks, the Romans, and the Saxons, and we, here in Europe, should not call a man educated or enlightened who was ignorant of the debt which he owes to his intellectual ancestors in Palestine, Greece, Rome, and Germany. The whole past history of the world would be darkness to him, and not knowing what those who came before him had done for him, he would probably care little to do anything for those who are to come after him. Life would be to him a chain of sand, while it ought to be a kind of electric chain that makes our hearts tremble and vibrate with the most ancient thoughts of the past, as well as with the most distant hopes of the future.

Let us begin with our religion. No one can understand even the historical possibility of the Christian religion without knowing something of the Jewish race, which must be studied chiefly in the pages of the *Old Testament*. And in order to appreciate the true relation of the Jews to the rest of ancient world, and to understand what ideas were peculiarly their own, and what ideas they shared in common with the other members of the Semitic stock, or what moral and religious impulses they received from the historical contact with other nations of antiquity, it is absolutely necessary that we should pay some attention to the history of Babylon, Nineveh, Phoenicia, and Persia. These may seem distant countries and forgotten people, and many might feel inclined to say, 'Let the dead bury their dead; what are those mummies to us?' Still, such is the marvellous continuity of history, that I could easily show you many things which we, even we who are here assembled, owe to Babylon, to Nineveh, to Egypt, Phoenicia, and Persia.

Every one who carries a watch, owes to the Babylonians the division of the hour into sixty minutes. It may be a very bad division, yet such as it is, it has come to us from the Greeks and Romans, and it came to them from Babylon. The sexagesimal division is peculiarly Babylonian. Hipparchos, 150 BC, adopted it from Babylon, Ptolemy, AD 150, gave it wider currency, and the French, when they decimalized everything else, respected the dial plates of our watches, and left them with their sixty Babylonian minutes.

Everyone who writes a letter, owes his alphabet to the Romans and Greeks; the Greeks owed their alphabet to the Phoenicians, and the Phoenicians learnt it in Egypt. It may be a very imperfect alphabet—as all the students of phonetics will tell you; yet, such as it is, and has been, we owe it to the old Phoenicians and Egyptians, and in every letter we trace, there lies imbedded the mummy of an ancient Egyptian hieroglyphic.

What do we owe to the Persians? It does not seem to be much, for they were not a very inventive race, and what they knew, they had chiefly learnt from their neighbours, the Babylonians and Assyrians. Still, we owe them something. First of all, we owe them a large debt of gratitude for having allowed themselves to be beaten by the Greeks; for think what the world would have been, if the Persians had beaten the Greeks at Marathon, and had enslaved, that means, annihilated, the genius of ancient Greece. However, this may be called rather an involuntary contribution to the progress of humanity, and I mention it only in order to show, how narrowly, not only Greeks and Romans, but Saxons and Anglo-Saxons too, escaped becoming Parsis or Fire-worshippers.

But I can mention at least one voluntary gift which came to us from Persia, and that is the relation of silver to gold in our bi-metallic currency. That relation was, no doubt, first determined in Babylonia, but it assumed its practical and historical importance in the Persian empire, and spread from there to the Greek colonies in Asia, and thence to Europe, where it has maintained itself with slight variation to the present day.

A *talent* was divided into sixty *mina*, a *mina* into sixty *shekels*. Here we have again the Babylonian sexagesimal system, a system which owes its origin and popularity, I believe, to the fact that *sixty* has the greatest number of divisors. *Shekel* was translated into Greek by *stater*, and an Athenian gold *stater*, like the Persian gold *stater*, down to the times of Croesus, Darius, and Alexander, was the sixtieth part of a *mina* of gold, not very far therefore from our sovereign. The proportion of silver to gold was fixed as 13 or $13\frac{1}{3}$ to 1; and if the weight of a silver *shekel* was made as 13 to 10, such a coin would correspond very nearly to our florin. Half a silver *shekel* was a *drachma*, and this was therefore the true ancestor of our shilling.

Again you may say that any attempt at fixing the relative value of silver and gold is, and always has been, a great mistake. Still it shows how closely the world is held together, and how, for good or for evil, we are what we are, not so much by ourselves as by the toil and moil of those who came before us, our true intellectual ancestors, whatever the blood may have been composed of that ran through their veins, or the bones which formed the rafters of their skulls.

And if it is true, with regard to religion, that no one could understand it and appreciate its full purpose without knowing its origin and growth, that is, without knowing something of what the cuneiform inscriptions of Mesopotamia, the hieroglyphic and hieratic texts of Egypt, and the historical monuments of Phoenicia and Persia can alone reveal to us, it is equally true with regard to all the other elements that constitute the whole of our intellectual life. If we are Jewish or Semitic in our religion, we are Greek in our philosophy, Roman in our politics, and Saxon in our morality, and it follows that a knowledge of the history of the Greeks, Romans, and Saxons, or of the flow of civilization from Greece to Italy, and through Germany to these isles, forms an essential element in what is called a liberal, that is, an historical and rational education.

But then it might be said. Let this be enough. Let us know by all means all that deserves to be known about our real spiritual ancestors in the great historical kingdoms of the world; let us be grateful for all we have inherited from Egyptians, Babylonians, Phoenicians, Jews, Greeks, Romans, and Saxons. But why bring in India? Why add a new burden to what every man has to bear already, before he can call himself fairly educated? What have we inherited from the dark dwellers on the Indus and the Ganges, that we should have to add their royal names and dates and deeds to the archives of our already overburdened memory?

There is some justice in this complaint. The ancient inhabitants of India are not our intellectual ancestors in the same direct way as Jews, Greeks, Romans, and Saxons are; but they represent, nevertheless, a collateral branch of that family to which we belong by language, that is, by thought, and their historical records extend in some respects so far beyond all other records and have been preserved to us in such perfect and such legible documents, that we can learn from them lessons which we can learn nowhere else, and supply missing links in our intellectual ancestry far more important than that missing link (which we can well afford to miss), the link between Ape and Man.

I am not speaking as yet of the literature of India as it is, but of something far more ancient, the language of India, or Sanskrit. No one supposes any longer that Sanskrit was the common source of Greek, Latin, and Anglo-Saxon. This used to be said, but it has long been shown that Sanskrit is only a collateral branch of the same stem from which spring Greek, Latin, and Anglo-Saxon; and not only these, but all the Teutonic, all the Celtic, all the Slavonic languages, nay, the languages of Persia and Armenia also.

What, then, is it that gives to Sanskrit its claim on our attention, and its supreme importance in the eyes of the historian?

First of all, its antiquity,—for we know Sanskrit at an earlier period than Greek. But what is far more important than its merely chronological antiquity is the antique state of preservation in which that Aryan language has been handed down to us. The world and known Latin and Greek for centuries, and it was felt, no doubt, that there was some kind of similarity between the two. But how was that similarity to be explained? Sometimes Latin was supposed to give the key to the formation of a Greek word, sometimes Greek seemed to betray the secret of the origin of a Latin word. Afterwards, when the ancient Teutonic languages, such as Gothic and Anglo-Saxon, and the ancient Celtic and Slavonic languages too, came to be studied, no one could help seeing a certain family likeness among them all. But how such a likeness between these languages came to be, and how, what is far more difficult to explain, such striking differences too between these languages came to be, remained a mystery, and gave rise to the most gratuitous theories, most of them, as you know, devoid of all scientific foundation. As soon, however, as Sanskrit stepped into the midst of these languages, there came light and warmth and mutual recognition. They all ceased to be strangers, and each fell of its own accord into its right place. Sanskrit was the eldest sister of them all, and could tell of many things which the other members of the family had quite forgotten. Still, the other languages too had each their own tale to tell; and it is out of all their tales together that a chapter in the human mind has been put together which, in some respects, is more important to us that any of the other chapters, the Jewish, the Greek, the Latin, or the Saxon.

The process by which that ancient chapter of history was recovered is very simple. Take the words which occur in the same form and with the same meaning in all the seven branches of the Aryan family, and you have in them the most genuine and trustworthy records in which to read the thoughts of our true ancestors, before they had become Hindus, or Persians, or Greeks, or Romans, or Celts, or

Teutons, or Slavs. Of course, some of these ancient charters may have been lost in one or other of these seven branches of the Aryan family, but even then, if they are found in six, or five, or four, or three, or even two only of its original branches, the probability remains, unless we can prove a later historical contact between these languages, that these words existed before the great *Aryan Separation.* If we find *agni,* meaning fire, in Sanskrit, and *ignis,* meaning fire, in Latin, we may safely conclude that *fire* was known to the undivided Aryans, even if no trace of the same name of fire occurred anywhere else. And why? Because there is no indication that Latin remained longer united with Sanskrit than any of the other Aryan languages, or that Latin could have borrowed such a word from Sanskrit, after these two languages had once become distinct. We have, however, the Lituanian *ugnis,* and the Scottish *ingle,* to show that the Slavonic and possibly the Teutonic languages also, knew the same word for fire, though they replaced it in time by other words. Words, like all other things, will die, and why they should live on in one soil and wither away and perish in another, is not always easy to say. What has become of *ignis,* for instance, in all the Romance languages? It has withered away and perished, probably because, after losing its final unaccentuated syllable, it became awkward to pronounce; and another word *focus,* which in Latin meant fire-place, hearth, altar, has taken its place.

Suppose we wanted to know whether the ancient Aryans before their separation knew the mouse: we should only have to consult the principal Aryan dictionaries, and we should find in Sanskrit *mush,* in Greek *mus* in Latin *mus,* in Old Slavonic *myse,* in Old High German *mus,* enabling us to say that, at a time so distant from us that we feel inclined to measure it by Indian rather than by our own chronology, the mouse was known, that is, was named, was conceived and recognised as a species of its own, not to be confounded with any other vermin.

And if we were to ask whether the enemy of the mouse, the *cat,* was known at the same at the same distant time, we should feel justified in saying decidedly, No. The cat is called in Sanskrit *marjara* and *vidala.* In Greek and Latin the words usually given as names of the cat, *galee* and *ailouros, mustella* and *felis,* did not originally signify the tame cat, but the weasel or marten. The name for the real cat in Greek was *katta,* in Latin *catus,* and these words have supplied the names for cat in all the Teutonic, Slavonic, and Celtic languages. The animal itself, so far as we know at present, came to Europe from Egypt, where it had been worshipped for centuries and tamed; and as this arrival probably dates from the fourth century AD, we can well understand that no common name for it could have existed when the Aryan nations separated.

In this way a more or less complete picture of the state of civilization, previous to the Aryan Separation, can be and has been reconstructed, like a mosaic put together with the fragments of ancient stones; and I doubt whether, in tracing the history of the human mind, we shall ever reach to a lower stratum than that which is revealed to us by the converging rays of the different Aryan languages.

Nor is that all; for even that Proto-Aryan language, as it has been reconstructed from the ruins scattered about in India, Greece, Italy, and Germany, is clearly the result of a long, long process of thought. One shrinks from chronological limitations when looking into such distant periods of life. But if we find Sanskrit as a perfect literary language, totally different from Greek and Latin, 1500 BC, where can those streams of Sanskrit, Greek, and Latin meet, as we trace them back to their common source? And then, when we have followed these mighty national streams back to their common meeting-point, even then that common language looks like a rock washed down and smoothed for ages by the ebb and flow of thought. We find in that language such a compound, for instance, as *asmi*, I am, Greek *esmi*. What would other languages give for such a pure concept as *I am*? They may say, *I stand*, or *I live*, or *I grow*, or *I turn*, but it is given to few languages only to be able to say *I am*. To us nothing seems more natural than the auxiliary verb *I am*: but, in reality, no work of art has required greater efforts than this little word *I am*. And all those efforts lie beneath the level of the common Proto-Aryan speech. Many different ways were open, were tried, too, in order to arrive at such a compound as *asmi*, and such a concept as *I am*. But all were given up, and this one alone remained, and was preserved for ever in all the languages and all the dialects of the Aryan family. In *as-mi* as is the root, and in the compound *as-mi*, the predicative root as, to be, is predicated of *mi*, I. But no language could ever produce at once so empty, or, if you like, so general a root as *as*, to be. *As* meant originally *to breathe*, and from it we have *asu*, breath, spirit, life, also *as* the mouth, Latin *os*, *oris*. By constant wear and tear this root *as*, to breathe, had first to lose all signs of its original material character, before it could convey that purely abstract meaning of existence, without any qualification, which has rendered to the higher operations of thought the same service which the nought, likewise the invention of Indian genius, has to render in arithmetic. Who will say how long the friction lasted which changed *as*, to breathe, into *as*, to be? And even a root *as*, to breathe, was an Aryan root, not Semitic, not Turanian. It possessed an historical individuality—it was the work of our forefathers, and represents a thread which unites us in our thoughts and words with those who first thought for us, with those who first spoke for us, and whose thoughts and words men are still thinking and speaking, though divided from them by thousands, it may be by hundreds of thousands of years.

This is what I call *history* in the true sense of the word, something really worth knowing, far more so than the scandals of courts, or the butcheries of nations, which fill so many pages of our Manuals of History. And all this work is only beginning, and whoever likes to labour in these the most ancient of historical archives will find plenty of discoveries to make—and yet people ask, what is the use of learning Sanskrit?

We get accustomed to everything, and cease to wonder at what would have startled our fathers and upset all their stratified notions, like a sudden earthquake. Every child now learns at school that English is an Aryan or Indo-European language, that it belongs to the Teutonic branch, and that this branch, together with the Italic, Greek, Celtic, Slavonic, Iranic, and Indic branches, all spring from the same stock, and form together the great Aryan or Indo-European family of speech.

But this, though it is taught now in our elementary schools, was really, but fifty years ago, like the opening of a new horizon of the world of the intellect, and the extension of a feeling of closest fraternity that made us feel at home where before we had been strangers, and changed millions of so-called barbarians into our own kith and kin. To speak the same language constitutes a closer union than to have drunk the same milk; and Sanskrit, the ancient language of India, is substantially the same language as Greek, Latin, and Anglo-Saxon. This is a lesson which we should never have learnt but from a study of Indian language and literature, and if India had taught us nothing else, it would have taught us more than almost any other language ever did.

It is quite amusing, though instructive also, to read what was written by scholars and philosophers when this new light first dawned on the world. They would not have it, they would not believe that there could be any community of origin between the people of Athens and Rome, and the so-called Niggers of India. The classical scholars scouted the idea, and I myself still remember the time, when I was a student at Leipzig and began to study Sanskrit, with what contempt any remarks on Sanskrit or comparative grammar were treated by my teachers, men such as Gottmed Hermann, Haupt, Westermann, Stallbaum, and others. No one ever was for a time so completely laughed down as Professor Bopp, when he first published his *Comparative Grammar of Sanskrit, Zend, Greek, Latin, and Gothic.* All hands were against him; and if in comparing Greek and Latin with Sanskrit, Gothic, Celtic, Slavonic, or Persian, he happened to have placed one single accent wrong, the shouts of those who knew nothing but Greek and Latin, and probably looked in their Greek dictionaries to be quite sure of their accents, would never end. Dugald Stewart, rather than admit a relationship between Hindus and Scots, would rather believe that the whole Sanskrit language and the whole of Sanskrit literature—mind, a literature extending over three thousand year and larger than the ancient literature of either Greece or Rome,—was a forgery of those wily priests, the Brahmans. I remember too how, when I was at school at Leipzig, (and a very good school it was, with such masters as Nobbe, Forbiger, Funkhaenel, and Palm,—an old school too, which could boast of Leibniz among its former pupils) I remember, I say, one of our masters (Dr. Klee) telling us one afternoon, when it was too hot to do any serious work, that there was a language spoken in India, which was much the same as Greek and Latin, nay, as German and Russian. At first we thought it was a joke, but when one saw the parallel columns of Numerals, Pronouns, and Verbs in Sanskrit, Greek, and Latin written on the black board, one felt in the presence of facts, before which one had to bow. All one's ideas of Adam and Eve, and the Paradise, and the tower of Babel, and Shem, Ham, and Japhet, with Homer and Æneas and Virgil too, seemed to be whirling round and round, till at last one picked up the fragments and tried to build up a new world, and to live with a new historical consciousness.

Here you will see why I consider a certain knowledge of India an essential portion of a liberal or an historical education. The concept of the European man has been changed and widely extended by our acquaintance with India, and we know now that we are something different from what we thought we were. Suppose the Americans, owing to some cataclysmal events, had forgotten their English origin, and after two or three thousand years found themselves in possession of a language and of ideas which they could trace back historically to a certain date, but which, at that date, seemed, as it were, fallen from the sky, without any explanation of their origin and previous growth, what would they say if suddenly the existence of an English language and literature were revealed to them, such as they existed in the seventh century—explaining all that seemed before almost miraculous, and solving almost every question that could be asked! Well, this is much the same as what the discovery of Sanskrit has done for us. It has added a new period to our historical consciousness, and revived the recollections of our childhood, which seemed to have vanished for ever.

Whatever else we may have been, it is quite clear now that, many thousands of years ago, we were something that had not yet developed into an Englishman, or a Saxon, or a Greek, or a Hindu either, yet contained in itself the germs of all these characters. A strange being, you may say. Yes, but for all that a year real being, and an ancestor too on whom we must learn to be proud, far more than of any such modern ancestors, as Normans, Saxons, Celts, and all the rest.

And this is not all yet that a study of Sanskrit and the other Aryan languages has done for us. It has not only widened our views of man, and taught us to embrace millions of strangers and barbarians as members of one family, but it has imparted to the whole ancient history of man a reality which it never possessed before.

We speak and write a great deal about antiquities, and if we can lay hold of a Greek statue or an Egyptian Sphinx or a Babylonian Bull, our heart rejoices, and we build museums grander than any Royal palaces to receive the treasures of the past. This is quite right. But are you aware that every one of us possesses what may be called the richest and most wonderful Museum of Antiquities, older than any statues, sphinxes, or bulls? And where? Why, in our own language. When I use such words as *father* or *mother*, *heart* or *tear, one, two, three, here* and *there.* I am handling coins or counters that were current before there was one single Greek statue, one single Babylonian Bull, one single Egyptian Sphinx. Yes, each of us carries about with him the richest and most wonderful Museum of Antiquities; and if he only knows how to treat those treasures, how to rub and polish them till they become translucent again, how to arrange them and read them, they will tell him marvels more marvellous than all hieroglyphics and cuneiform inscriptions put together. The stories they have told us are beginning to be old stories now. Many of you have heard them before. But do not let them cease to be marvels, like so many things which cease to be marvels because they happen every day. And do not think that there is nothing left for you to do. There are more marvels still to be discovered in language than have ever been revealed to us; nay, there is no word, however common, if only you know how to take it to pieces, like a cunningly contrived work of art, fitted together thousands of years ago by the most cunning of artists, the human mind, that will not make you listen and marvel more than any chapter of the *Arabian Nights.*

But I must not allow myself to be carried away from my proper subject. All I wish to impress on you by way of introduction is that the results of the Science of Language, which, without the aid of Sanskrit, would never have been obtained, form an essential element of what we call a liberal, that is an historical education,—an education which will enable a man to do what the French call *s'orienter,* that is, 'to find his East,' 'his true East,' and thus to determine his real place in the world; to know, in fact, the port whence man started, the course he has followed, and the port towards which he has to steer.

We all come from the East—all that we value most has come to us from the East, and in going to the East, not only those who have received a special Oriental training, but everybody who has enjoyed the advantages of a liberal, that is, of a truly historical education, ought to feel that he is going to his 'old home,' full of memories, if only he can read them. Instead of feeling your hearts sink within you, when next year you approach the shores of India, I wish that every one of you could feel what Sir William Jones felt, when, just one hundred years ago, he came to the end of his long voyage from England, and saw the shores of India rising on the horizon. At that time young men going to the wonderland of India, were not ashamed of dreaming dreams, and seeing visions: and this was the dream dreamt and the vision seen by Sir William Jones:

'When I was at sea last August (that is in August, 1783), on my voyage to this country (India) I had long and ardently desired to visit, I found one evening, on inspecting the observations of the day, that *India* lay before us, *Persia* on our left, whilst a breeze from *Arabia* blew nearly on our stern. A situation so pleasing in itself and to me so new, could not fail to awaken a train of reflections in a mind, which had early been accustomed to contemplate with delight the eventful histories and agreeable fictions of this Eastern world. It gave me inexpressible pleasure to find myself in the midst of so noble an amphitheatre, almost encircled by the vast regions of Asia, which has ever been esteemed the nurse of sciences, the inventress of delightful and useful arts, the scene of glorious actions, fertile in the productions of human genius, and infinitely diversified in the forms of religion and government, in the laws, manners, customs and languages, as well as in the features and complexions of men. I could not help remarking how important and extensive a field was yet unexplored, and how many solid advantages unimproved.'

India wants more such dreamers as Sir William Jones, then 37 years of age, standing alone on the deck of his vessel and watching the sun diving into the sea—with the memories of England behind and the hopes of India before him, feeling the presence of Persia and its ancient monarchs, and breathing the breezes af Arabia and its glowing poetry. Such dreamers know how to make their dreams come true, and how to change their visions into realities.

And as it was a hundred years ago, so it is now; or at least, so it may be now. There are many bright dreams to be dreamt about India, and many bright deeds to be done in India, if only you will do them. Though many great and glorious conquests have been made in the history and literature of the East, since the days when Sir William Jones landed at Calcutta, depend upon it, no young Alexander here need despair because there are no kingdoms left for him to conquer on the ancient shores of the Indus and the Ganges.

Notes

Pages

3. **Marco Polo:** 'The first traveller to cross the entire continent of Asia'; late 13th century AD; his observations on South Indian Kingdoms are very valuable. His travel diary has been translated into English more than once.
Elephanta: A famous set of cave temples on an island six miles from Bombay. The name Elephanta is due to the Portuguese, who were apparently struck by the stone elephants which were once found in the landing place.
Towers of Silence: On which Parsis expose dead bodies that they may be devoured by vultures, as required by their religion.
Sir William Jones (1746-1794): became judge of the Supreme Court at Calcutta in 1783. He was the first English scholar to study Sanskrit. Founder and first President of the Asiatic Society of Bengal, established 1784.

Thomas Colebrooke (1765-1837): A great mathematician and astronomer, and a profound Sanskrit scholar. Judge of the Sadr Diwani Adalat in 1801, and head of that court four years later; member of the Supreme Council from 1807 to 1812, and then of the Board of Revenue till the close of 1814 when he returned to England: President of the Asiatic Society of Bengal (1807-14). Helped at the foundation of the Royal Asiatic Society, London, in 1823, and became its Director.

5. **Hooker** (William Jackson, 1785-1865): English botanist; director of the Botanical Garden of Kew, London.

   Haeckel (Ernst Heinrich, 1834-1919): German biologist who published an account of his Indian travels in 1882. The first to draw up a genealogical tree of the relationship between the various orders of animals.

6. **Darics** : Old Persian gold coins bearing the effigy of Darius.

   Plato's Cratylus: Cratylus, 411 A. 'Still as I have put on the lion's skin, I must not be faint-hearted.' Possibly, however, this may refer to Hercules, and not to the fable of the donkey in the lion's or the tiger's skin. In the *Hitopadesa,* a donkey, being nearly starved, is sent by his master into a cornfield to feed. In order to shield him he put a tiger's skin on him. All goes well till a watchman approaches, hiding himself under his grey coat, and trying to shoot the tiger. The donkey thinks it is a grey female donkey, begins to bray, and is killed. (M.M.)

7. **Judgment of Solomon:** I Kings, iii, 16 ff.

   Tripitaka: means literally 'three baskets'. A name applied to the Canonical Literature of Buddhism collected in three sections : Vinaya, discipline; Sutra, religious instruction; and Abhidharma, metaphysics.

18. **Bopp** : (Franz, 1791-1867): German philologist who first developed the scientific principles of Indo-European philology in the work mentioned by Max Müller.

    Dugald Stewart: Professor of Moral Philosophy at Edinburgh, 1785-1810.

LECTURE II

Character of the Hindus

IN my first lecture I endeavoured to remove the prejudice that everything in India is strange, and so different from the intellectual life which we are accustomed to in England that the twenty or twenty-five years which a Civil servant has to spend in the East seem often to him a kind of exile that he must bear as well as he can, but that severs him completely from all those higher pursuits by which life is made enjoyable at home. This need not be so and ought not to be so, if only it is clearly seen how almost every one of the higher interests that make life worth living here in England, may find as ample scope in India as in England.

Today I shall have to grapple with another prejudice which is even more mischievous. Because it forms a kind of icy barrier between the Hindus and their rulers, and makes anything like a feeling of true fellowship between the two utterly impossible.

That prejudice consists in looking upon our stay in India as a kind of *moral* exile, and in regarding the Hindus as an inferior race, totally different from ourselves in their moral character, and, more particularly in what forms the very foundation of the English character, respect for truth.

I believe there is nothing more disheartening to any high-minded young man than the idea that he will have to spend his life among human beings whom he can never respect or love—natives, as they are called, not to use even more offensive names—men whom he is taught to consider as not amenable, he recognised principles of self respect, uprightness, and veracity, and with whom therefore any community of interests and action, much more any real friendship, is supposed to be out of the question.

So often has that charge of untruthfulness been repeated, and so generally is it now accepted, that it seems almost Quixotic to try to fight against it.

Nor should I venture to fight this almost hopeless battle, if I were not convinced that such a charge, like all charges brought against a whole nation, rests on the most flimsy induction, and that it has done, is doing, and will continue to do more mischief than anything that even the bitterest enemy of English dominion in India could have invented. If a young man who goes to India as a Civil servant or as a military officer, goes there fully convinced that the people whom he is to meet with are all liars, liars by nature or by national instinct, never restrained in their dealings by any regard for truth, never to be trusted on their word, need we wonder at the feelings of disgust with which he thinks of the Hindus, even before he has seen them; the feelings of distrust with which he approaches them, and the contemptuous way in which he treats them when brought into contact with them for the transaction of public or private business? When such tares have once been sown by the enemy, it will be difficult to gather them up. It has become almost an article of faith with every Indian Civil servant that all Indians are liars; nay, I know, I shall never be forgiven for my heresy in venturing to doubt it.

Now, quite apart from India, I feel most strongly that every one of these international condemnations should be deprecated, not only for the sake of the self-conceited and uncharitable state of mind from which they spring, and which they serve to strengthen and confirm, but for purely logical reasons also, namely for the reckless and slovenly character of the induction on which such conclusions rest. Because a man has travelled in Greece and has been cheated by his dragoman, or been carried off by brigands, does it follow that all Greeks, ancient as well as modern, are cheats and robbers, or that they approve of cheating and robbery? And because in Calcutta, or Bombay, or Madras, Indians who are brought before judges, or who hang about the law courts and the bazaars are not distinguished by an unreasoning and uncompromising love of truth, is it not a very vicious induction to say, in these days of careful reasoning, that all Hindus are liars—particularly if you bear in mind that the number of inhabitants of that vast country amounts to hundreds of millions. Are all these many millions of human beings to be set down as liars, because some hundreds, say even some thousands of Indians, when they are brought before an English court of law, on suspicion of having committed a theft or a murder, do not speak the truth, the whole truth, and nothing but the truth? Would an English sailor, if brought before a dark-skinned judge, who spoke English with a strange accent, how down before him and confess at once any misdeed that he may have committed; and would all his mates rush forward and eagerly bear witness against him, when he had got himself into trouble?

The rules of induction are general, but they depend on the subjects to which they are applied. We may, to follow an Indian proverb, judge of a whole field of rice by tasting one or two grains only, but if we apply this rule to human beings, we are sure to fall into the same mistake as the English chaplain who had once, on board an English vessel, christened a French child, and who remained fully convinced for the rest of his life that all French babies had very long noses.

I can hardly think of anything that you could safely predicate of *all* the inhabitants of India, and I confess to a little nervous tremor whenever I see a sentence beginning with 'The people of India,' or even with 'All the Brahmans,' or 'All the Buddhists.' What follows is almost invariably wrong. There is a greater difference between an Afghan, a Sikh, a Rajput, a Bengali, and a Dravidian than between an Englishman, a Frenchman, a German, and a Russian—yet all are classed as Hindus, and all are supposed to fall under the same sweeping condemnation.

Let me read you what Sir John Malcolm says about the diversity of character to be observed by any one who has eyes to observe, among the different races whom we promiscuously call Hindus, and whom we promiscuously condemn as Hindus. After describing the people of Bengal as weak in body and timid in mind, and those below Calcutta as the lowest of our Hindu subjects, both in character and appearance, he continues: 'But from the moment you enter the district of Behar, the Hindu inhabitants are a race of men, generally speaking, not more distinguished by their lofty stature and robust frame than they are for some of the finest qualities of the mind. They are brave, generous, humane, and their truth is as remarkable as their courage.'

But because I feel bound to protest against the indiscriminate abuse that has been heaped on the people of India from the Himalaya to Ceylon, do not suppose that it is my wish or intention to draw an ideal picture of India, leaving out all the dark shades, and giving you nothing but 'sweetness and light.' Having never been in India myself, I can only claim for myself the right and duty of every historian, namely, the right of collecting as much information as possible, and the duty to sift it according to the recognised rules of historical criticism. My chief sources of information with regard to the national character of the Indians in ancient times will be the works of Greek writers and the literature of the ancient Indians themselves. For later times we must depend on the statements of the various conquerors of India, who are not always the most lenient judges of those whom they may find it more difficult to rule than to conquer. For the last century to the present day, I shall have to appeal, partly to the authority of those who, after spending an active life in India and among the Indians, have given us the benefit of their experience in published works; partly to the testimony of a number of distinguished Civil servants and of Indian gentlemen also, whose personal acquaintance I have enjoyed in England, in France, and in Germany.

As I have chiefly to address myself to those who will themselves be the rulers and administrators of India in the future, allow me to begin with the opinions which some of the most eminent, and, I believe, the most judicious among the Indian civil servants of the past have formed and deliberately expressed on the point which we are today discussing, namely, the veracity or want of veracity among the Hindus.

And here I must begin with a remark which has been made by others also, namely, that the Civil servants who went to India in the beginning of this century, and under the auspices of the old East-India Company, many of whom I had the honour and pleasure of knowing when I first came to England, seemed to have seen a great deal more of native life, native manners, and native character than those whom I had to examine five-and-twenty years ago, and who are now, after a distinguished career, coming back to England. India is no longer the distant island which it was, where each Crusoe had to make a home for himself as best he could. With the short and easy voyages from England to India and from India to England, with the frequent mails, and the telegrams, and the Anglo-Indian newspapers, official life in India has assumed the character of a temporary exile rather, which even English ladies are now more ready to share than fifty years ago. This is a difficulty which cannot be removed, but must be met, and which, I believe, can best be met by inspiring the new Civil servants with new and higher interests during their stay in India.

I knew the late Professor Wilson, our Boden Professor of Sanskrit at Oxford, for many years, and often listened with deep interest to his Indian reminiscences.

Let me read you what he, Professor Wilson, says of his native friends, associates, and servants:

'I lived, both from necessity and choice, very much amongst the Hindus, and had opportunities of becoming acquainted with them in a greater variety of situations than those in which they usually come under the observation of Europeans. In the Calcutta mint, for instance, I was in daily personal communication with a numerous body of artificers, mechanics, and labourers, and always found amongst them cheerful and unwearied industry, good-humoured compliance with the will of their superiors, and a readiness to make whatever exertions were demanded from them: there was among them no drunkenness, no disorderly conduct, no insubordination. It would not be true to say that there was *no* dishonesty, but it was comparatively rare, invariably petty, and much less formidable than, I believe, it is necessary to guard against in other mints in other countries. There was considerable skill and ready docility. So far from there being any servility, there was extreme frankness, and I should say that where there is confidence without fear, frankness is one of the most universal features in the Indian character. Let the people feel sure of the temper and good-will of their superiors, and there is an end of reserve and timidity, without the slightest departure from respect . . . .'

Then, speaking of the much-abused Indian Pandits, he says: 'The studies which engaged my leisure brought me into connection with the men of learning, and in them I found the similar merits of industry, intelligence, cheerfulness, frankness, with others peculiar to their avocation. A very common characteristic of these men, and of the Hindus especially was a simplicity truly childish, and a total unacquaintance with the business and manners of life. Where that feature was lost, it was chiefly by those who had been long familiar with Europeans. Amongst the Pandits, or the learned Hindus, there prevailed great ignorance and great dread of the European character. There is, indeed, very little intercourse between any class of Europeans and Hindu scholars, and it is not wonderful, therefore, that mutual mis-apprehension should prevail.'

Speaking, lastly, of the higher classes in Calcutta and elsewhere. Professor Wilson says that he witnessed among them 'polished manners, clearness and comprehensiveness of understanding, liberality of feeling and independence of principle that would have stamped them gentlemen in any country in the world.' 'With some of this class,' he adds, 'I formed friendships which I trust to enjoy through life.'

I have often heard Professor Wilson speak in the same, and in even stronger terms of his old friends in India, and his correspondence with Ram Comul Sen, the grandfather of Keshub Chunder Sen, a most orthodox, not to say bigoted, Hindu, which has lately been published, shows on what intimate terms Englishmen and Hindus may be, if only the advances are made on the England side.

There is another Professor of Sanskrit, of whom your University may well be proud, and who could speak on this subject with far greater authority than I can. He too will tell you, and I have no doubt has often told you, that if only you look out for friends among the Hindus, you will find them, and you may trust them.

There is one book which for many years I have been in the habit of recommending, and another against which I have always been warning those of the candidates for the Indian Civil Service whom I happened to see at Oxford: and I believe both the advice and the warning have in several cases borne the very best fruit. The book which I consider most mischievous, nay, which I hold responsible for some of the greatest misfortunes that have happened to India, is Mill's *History of British India,* even with the antidote against its poison, which is supplied by Professor Wilson's notes. The book which I recommend, and which I wish might be published again in a cheaper form, so as to make it more generally accessible, is Colonel Sleeman's *Rambles and Recollections of an Indian Official,* published in 1844, but written originally in 1835-36.

Mill's *History,* no doubt, you all know, particularly the candidates for the Indian Civil Service, who, I am sorry to say, are recommended to read it and are examined in it. Still, in order to substantiate my strong condemnation of the book, I shall have to give a few proofs:

Mill in his estimate of the Hindu character is chiefly guided by Dubois, a French missionary, and by Orme and Buchanan, Tennant, and Ward, all of them neither very competent nor very unprejudiced judges. Mill, however, picks out all that is most unfavourable from their works, and omits the qualifications which even these writers felt bound to give to their wholesale condemnation of the Hindus. He quotes as serious, for instance, what was said in joke, namely, that 'a Brahman is an ant's nest of lies and impostures.' Next to the charge of untruthfulness, Mill upbraids the Hindus for what he calls their litigiousness. He writes: 'As often as courage fails them in seeking more daring gratification to their hatred and revenge their malignity finds a vent in the channel of litigation.' Without imputting dishonourable motives, as Mill does, the same fact might be stated in a different way, by saying, 'As often as their conscience and respect of law keep them from seeking more daring gratification to their hatred and revenge, say by murder or poisoning, their trust in English justice leads them to appeal to our Courts of Law.' Dr. Robertson, in his *Historical Disquisitions concerning India*, seems to have considered the litigious subtlety of the Hindus as a sign of high civilization rather than of barbarism, but he is sharply corrected by Mr. Mill, who tells him that 'nowhere is this subtlety carried higher than among the wildest of the Irish.' That courts of justice in which a verdict was not to be obtained, as formerly, by bribes and corruption, should at first have proved very attractive to the Hindus, need not surprise us. But is it really true that the Hindus are more fond of litigation than other nations? If we consult Sir Thomas Munro, the eminent Governor of Madras, and the powerful advocate of the Ryotwar settlements, he tells us in so many words: 'I have had ample opportunity of observing the Hindus in every situation, and I can affirm, that they are not litigious.'

But Mill goes further still, and in one place he actually assures his readers that a 'Brahman may put a man to death when he lists.' In fact, he represents the Hindus as such a monstrous mass of all vices that, as Colonel Vans Kennedy remarked, society could not have held together, if it had really consisted of such reprobates only. Nor does he seem to see the full bearing of his remarks. Surely, if a Brahman might, as he says, put a man to death whenever he lists, it would be the strongest testimony in their favour that you hardly ever hear of their availing themselves of such a privilege, to say nothing of the fact—and a fact it is—that, according to statistics, the number of capital sentences was one in every 10,000 in England, but only one in every million in Bengal.

Colonel Sleeman's *Rambles* are less known than they deserve to be. To give you an idea of the man, I must read you some extracts from the book.

His sketches being originally addressed to his sister, this is how he writes to her:

'My dear Sister,

'Were anyone to ask your countrymen in India, what had been their greatest source of pleasure while there, perhaps, nine in ten would say, the letters which they receive from their sisters at home .... And while thus contributing so much to our happiness, they no doubt tend to make us better citizens of the world, and servants of government, than we should otherwise be; for in our "struggles through life" in India, we have all, more or less, an eye to the approbation of those circles which our kind sisters represent,—who may therefore be considered in the exalted light of a valuable species of *unpaid magistracy* to the government of India.'

There is a touch of the old English chivalry even in these few words addressed to a sister whose approbation he values, and with whom he hoped to spend the winter of his life. Having been, as he confesses, idle in answering letters, or rather, too busy to find time for long letters, he made use of his enforced leisure, while on his way from the Narmada river to the Himalaya mountains, in search of health, to give to his sister a full account of his impressions and experiences in India. Though what he was intended at first 'to interest and amuse his sister only and the other members of his family at home,' he adds in a more serious tone: 'Of one thing I must beg you to be assured, that I have nowhere indulged in fiction, either in the narrative, the recollections, or the conversations. What I relate on the testimony of others, I believe to be true: and what I relate on my own, you may rely upon as being so.'

When placing his volumes before the public at large in 1844, he expresses a hope that they may 'tend to make the people of India better understood by those of our countrymen whose destinies are cast among them, and inspire more kindly feelings towards them.'

You may ask why I consider Colonel Sleeman so trustworthy an authority on the Indian character, more trustworthy, for instance, than even so accurate and unprejudiced an observer as Professor Wilson. My answer is—because Wilson lived chiefly in Calcutta, while Colonel Sleeman saw India, where alone the true India can be seen, namely, in the village-communities. For many years he was employed as Commissioner for the suppression of Thuggee. The Thuggs were professional assassins, who committed their murders under a kind of religious sanction. They were originally 'all Mohammedans, but for a long time past Mohammedans and Hindus had been indiscriminately associated in the gangs, the former class, however, still predominating.'

In order to hunt up these gangs, Colonel Sleeman had constantly to live among the people in the country, to gain their confidence, and to watch the good as well as the bad features in their character.

Now what Colonel Sleeman continually insists on is that no one knows the Indians who does not know them in their village-communities—what we should now call their *communes.* It is that village in which India has given its peculiar impress to the Indian character, more so than in any other country we know. When in Indian history we hear so much of kings and emperors, of rajahs and maharajahs, we are apt to think of India as an Eastern monarchy, ruled by a central power, and without any trace of that self-government which forms the pride of England. But those who have most carefully studied the political life of India tell you the very opposite.

The political unit, or the social cell in India has always been, and, in spite of repeated foreign conquests, is still the village-community. Some of these political units will occasionally combine or be combined for common purposes (such a confederacy being called a Gramajala), but each is perfect in itself. When we read in the laws of Manu of officers appointed to rule over ten, twenty, a hundred, or a thousand of these villages, that means no more than that they were responsible for the collection of taxes, and generally for the good behaviour of these villages. And when, in later times, we hear of circles of 84 villages, the so-called Chourasees, and of 360 villages, this too seems to refer to fiscal arrangements only. To the ordinary Hindu, I mean to ninety-nine in every hundred, the village was his world, and the sphere of public opinion, with its beneficial influences on individuals, seldom extended beyond the horizon of his village.

Colonel Sleeman was one of the first who called attention to the existence of these village-communities in India, and their importance in the social fabric of the whole country both in ancient and in modern times; and though they have since become far better known and celebrated through the writings of Sir Henry Maine, it is still both interesting and instructive to read Colonel Sleeman's account. He writes as a mere observer, and uninfluenced as yet by any theories on the development of early social and political life among the Aryan nations in general.

I do not mean to say that Colonel Sleeman was the first who pointed out the palpable fact that the whole of India is parcelled out into estates of villages. Even so early an observer as Megasthenes seems to have been struck by the same fact when he says that 'in India the husbandmen with their wives and children live in the country, and entirely avoid going into town.' Nearchus observed that families cultivated the soil in common. What Colonel Sleeman was the first to point out was that all the native virtues of the Hindus are intimately connected with their village-life.

That village-life, however, is naturally the least known to English officials, nay, the very presence of an English official is often said to be sufficient to drive away those native virtues which distinguish both the private life and the public administration of justice and equity in an Indian village. Take a man out of his village-community, and you remove him from all the restraints of society. He is out of his element, and, under temptation, is more likely to go wrong than to remain true to the traditions of his home-life. Even between village and village the usual restraints of public morality are not always recognised. What would be called theft or robbery at home, is called a successful raid or conquest if directed against distant villages; and what would be falsehood or trickery in private life is honoured by the name of policy and diplomacy if successful against strangers. On the other hand, the rules of hospitality applied only to people of other villages, and a man of the same village could never claim the right of an *Atithi*, or guest.

Let us hear now what Colonel Sleeman tells us about the moral character of the members of these village-communities, and let us not forget that the Commissioner for the suppression of Thuggee had ample opportunities of seeing the dark as well as the bright side of the Indian character.

He assures us that falsehood or lying between members of the same village is almost unknown. Speaking of some of the most savage tribes, the Gonds, for instance, he maintains that nothing would induce them to tell a lie, though they would think nothing of lifting a heard of cattle from a neighbouring plain.

Of these men it might perhaps be said that they have not yet learned the value of a lie; yet even such blissful ignorance ought to count in a nation's favour. But I am not pleading here for Gonds, or Bhils, or Santhals, and other non-Aryan tribes. I am speaking of the Aryan and more or less civilized inhabitants of India. Now among them, where rights, duties, and interests begin to clash in one and the same village, public opinion, in its limited sphere, seems strong enough to deter even an evil-disposed person from telling a falsehood. The fear of the gods also has not yet lost its power. In most villages there is a sacred tree, a pipal tree (*Ficus Indica*), and the gods are supposed to delight to sit among its leaves, and listen to the music of their rustling. The deponent takes one of these leaves in his hand, and invokes the god, who sits above him, to crush him, or those dear to him, as he crushes the leaf in his hand, if he speaks anything but the truth. He then plucks and crushes the leaf, and states what he has to say.

The pipal tree is generally supposed to be occupied by one of the Hindu deities, while the large cotton-tree, particularly among the wilder tribes, is supposed to be the abode of local gods, all the more terrible, because entrusted with the police of a small settlement only. In their panchayats, Sleeman tells us, men adhere habitually and religiously to the truth, and 'I have had before me hundreds of cases,' he says, 'in which a man's property, liberty, and life has depended upon his telling a lie, and he has refused to tell it.'

Could many an English judge say the same?

In their own tribunals under the pipal-tree or cotton-tree, imagination commonly did what the deities, who were supposed to preside, had the credit of doing. If the deponent told a lie, he believed that the god who sat on his sylvan throne above him, and searched the heart of man, must know it; and from that moment he knew no rest, he was always in dread of his vengeance. If any accident happened to him, or to those dear to him, it was attributed to this offended deity; and if no accident happened, some evil was brought about by his own disordered imagination. It was an excellent superstition, inculcated in the ancient law-books, that the ancestors watched the answer of a witness, because, according as it was true or false, they themselves would go to heaven or to hell.

Allow me to read you the abstract of a conversation between an English official and a native law-officer as reported by Colonel Sleeman. The native lawyer was asked what he thought would be the effect of an act to dispense with oaths on the *Koran* and Ganges-water, and to substitute a solemn declaration made in the name of God, and under the same penal liabilities as if the *Koran* or Ganges-water had been in the deponent's hand.

'I have practised in the courts,' the native said, 'for thirty years, and during that time I have found only three kinds of witnesses—two of whom would, by such an act, be left precisely where they were, while the third would be released by it from a very salutary check.'

'And, pray, what are the three classes into which you divide the witnesses in our courts?'

'First, Sir, are those who will always tell the truth, whether they are required to state what they know in the form of an oath or not.'

'Do you think this a large class?'

'Yes, I think it is; and I have found among them many whom nothing on earth could make to swerve from the truth. Do what you please, you could never frighten or bribe them into a deliberate falsehood.

'The second are those who will not hesitate to tell a lie when they have a motive for it, and are not restrained by an oath. In taking an oath, they are afraid of two things, the anger of God, and the odium of men.

'Only three days ago,' he continued, 'I required a power of attorney from a lady of rank, to enable me to act for her in a case pending before the court in this town. It was given to me by her brother, and two witnesses came to declare that she had given it. "Now," said I, "this lady is known to live under the curtain, and you will be asked by the judge whether you saw her give this paper: what will you say?" They both replied—"If the judge asks us the question without an oath we will say '*Yes*'—it will save much trouble, and we know that she *did* give the paper, though we did not really *see* her give it; but if he puts the *Koran* into our hands, we must say '*No*', for we should otherwise be pointed at by all the town as perjured wretches—our enemies would soon tell everybody that we had taken a false oath."

'Now,' the native lawyer went on, 'the form of an oath is a great check on this sort of persons.

'The third class consists of men who will tell lies whenever they have a sufficient motive, whether they nave the *Koran* or Ganges-water in their hand or not. Nothing will ever prevent their doing so; and the declaration which you propose would be just as well as any other for them.'

'Which class do you consider the most numerous of the three?'

'I consider the second the most numerous, and wish the oath to be retained for them.'

'That is, of all the men you see examined in our courts, you think the most come under the class of those who will, under the influence of strong motives, tell lies, if they have not the *Koran* or Ganges-water in their hands?'

'Yes.'

'But do not a great many of those whom you consider to be

included among the second class come from the village-communities,—the peasantry of the country?'

'Yes.'

'And do you not think that the greatest part of those men who will tell lies in the court, under the influence of strong motives, unless they have the *Koran* or Ganges-water in their hands, would refuse to tell lies, if questioned before the people of their villages, among the circle in which they live?'

'Of course I do; three-fourth of those who do not scruple to lie in the courts, would be ashamed to lie before their neighbours, or the elders of their village.'

'You think that the people of the village-communities are more ashamed to tell lies before their neighbours than the people of towns?'

'Much more—there is no comparison.'

'And the people of towns and cities bear in India but a small proportion to the people of the village-communities?'

'I should think a very small proportion indeed.'

'Then you think that in the mass of the population of India, *out of our courts*, the first class, or those who speak truth, whether they have the *Koran* or Ganges-water in their hands or not, would be found more numerous than the other two?'

'Certainly I do; if they were always to be questioned before their neighbours or elders, so that they could feel that their neighbours and elders could know what they say.'

It was from a simple sense of justice that I felt bound to quote this testimony of Colonel Sleeman as to the truthful character of the natives of India, when *left to themselves*. My interest lies altogether with the people of India, *when left to themselves*, and historically I should like to draw a line after the year one thousand after Christ.

Now, it is quite true that during the two thousand years which precede the time of Mahmud of Gazni, India has had but few foreign visitors, and few foreign critics; still it is surely extremely strange that whenever, either in Greek, or in Chinese, or in Persian, or in Arab writings, we meet with any attempts at describing the distinguishing features in the national character of the Indians, regard for truth and justice should always be mentioned first.

Ktesias, the famous Greek physician of Artaxerxes Mnemon (present at the battle of Cunaxa, 404 BC), the first Greek writer who tells us anything about the character of the Indians, such as he heard it described at the Persian court, has a special chapter 'On the justice of the Indians.'

Megasthenes, the ambassador of Seleucus Nicator at the court of Sandrocottus in Palibothra (Pataliputra, the modern Patna), states that thefts were extremely rare, and that they honoured truth and virtue.

Arrian (in the second century, the pupil of Epictetus), when speaking of the public overseers or superintendents in India, says: 'They oversee what goes on in the country or towns, and report everything to the king, where the people have a king, and to the magistrates, where the people are self-governed, and it is against use and wont for these to give in a false report; *but indeed no Indian is accused of lying.*'

The Chinese, who come next in order of time, bear the same, I believe, unanimous testimony in favour of the honesty and veracity of the Hindus. Let me quote Hiuen-tsang, the most famous of the Chinese Buddhist pilgrims, who visited India in the seventh century. 'Though the Indians,' he writes, 'are of a light temperament, they are distinguished by the straightforwardness and honesty of their character. With regard to riches, they never take anything unjustly; with regard to justice, they make even excessive concessions .... Straightforwardness is the distinguishing feature of their administration.'

If we turn to the account given by the Mohammedan conquerors of India, we find Idrisi, in his *Geography* (written in the 11th century), summing up their opinion of the Indians in the following words:

'The Indians are naturally inclined to justice, and never depart from it in their action. Their good faith, honesty, and fidelity to their engagements are well known, and they are so famous for these qualities that people flock to their country from every side.'

Again in the thirteenth century, Shems-ed-din Abu Abdallah quotes the following judgment of Bedi ezr Zenân: 'The Indians are innumerable, like grains of sand, free from all deceit and violence. They fear neither death nor life.'

In the same century we have also the testimony of Marco Polo, who thus speaks of the Abraiaman, a name by which he seems to mean the Brahmans who, though not traders by profession, might well have been employed for great commercial transaction by the king. This was particularly the case during times which the Brahmans would call times of distress, when many things were allowed which at other times were forbidden by the laws. 'You must know.' Marco Polo says, 'that these Abraiaman are the best merchants in the world, and the most truthful, for they would not tell a lie for anything on earth.'

In the fourteenth century we have Friar Jordanus, who goes out of his way to tell us that the people of Lesser India (South and Western India) are true in speech and eminent in justice.

In the fifteenth century Kamal-eddin Abd-errazak Samarkandi (1413-82), who went as ambassador of the Khakan to the prince of Kalikut and to the King of Vijayanagara (about 1440-45), bears testimony to the perfect security which merchants enjoy in that country.

In the sixteenth century, Abul Fazl, the minister of the Emperor Akbar, says in his *Ain-i-Akbari:* 'The Hindus are religious, affable, cheerful, lovers of justice, given to retirement, able in business, admirers of truth, grateful and of unbounded fidelity; and their soldiers know not what it is to fly from the field of battle.'

And even in quite modern times the Mohammedans seem willing to admit that the Hindus, at all events in their dealings with Hindus, are more straightforward than Mohammedans in their dealings with Mohammedans.

Thus Meer Sulamut Ali, venerable old Mussulman, and, as Colonel Sleeman says, a most valuable public servant, was obliged to admit that 'a Hindu may feel himself authorised to take in a Mussulman, and might even think it meritorious to do so; but he would never think it meritorious to take in one of his own religion. There are no less than seventy-two sects of Mohammedans; and every one of these sects would not only take in the followers of every other religion on earth, but every member of every one of the other seventy-one sects; and the nearer that sect is to his own, the greater the merit of taking in its members.'

So I could go on quoting from book after book, and again and again we should see how it was love of truth that struck all the people who came in contact with India, as the prominent feature in the national character of its inhabitants. No one ever accused them of falsehood. There must surely be some ground for this, for it is not remark that is frequently made be travellers in foreign countries, even in our time, that their inhabitants invariably speak the truth. Read the accounts of English travellers in France, and you will find very little said about French honesty and veracity, while French accounts of England are seldom without a fling at *Perfide Albion*!

But if all this is true, how is it, you may well ask, that public opinion in England is so decidedly unfriendly to the people of India; at the utmost tolerates and patronizes them, but will never trust them, never treat them on terms of equality?

I have already hinted at some of the reasons. Public opinion with regard to India is made up in England chiefly by those who have spent their lives in Calcutta, Bombay, Madras, or some other of the principal towns in India. The native element in such towns contains mostly the most unfavourable specimens of the Indian population. An insight into the domestic life of the more respectable classes, even in towns, is difficult to obtain; and, when it is obtained, it is extremely difficult to judge of their manners according to our standard of what is proper, respectable, or gentleman-like. The misunderstandings are frequent and often most grotesque; and such, we must confess, is human nature, that when we hear the different and often very conflicting accounts of the character of the Hindus, many of us are rather sceptical with regard to unsuspected virtues among them, while we are quite disposed to accept unfavourable accounts of their character.

Lest I should seem to be pleading too much on the native side of the question, and to exaggerate the difficulty of forming a correct estimate of the character of the Hindus, let me appeal to one of the most distinguished, learned, and judicious members of the Indian Civil Service, the author of the *History of India,* Mountstuart Elphinstone. 'Englishmen in India,' he says, 'have less opportunity than might be expected of forming opinions of the native character. Even in England, few know much of the people beyond their own class, and what they do know, they learn from newspapers and publications of a description which does not exist in India. In that country also, religion and manners put bars to our intimacy with the natives, and limit the number of transactions as well as the free communication of opinions. We know nothing of the interior of families but by report, and have no share in those numerous occurrences of life in which the amiable parts of character are most exhibited.' 'Missionaries of a different religion, judges, police-magistrates, officers of revenue or customs, and even diplomatists, do not see the most virtuous portion of a nation, nor any portion, unless when influenced by passion, or occupied by some personal interest. What we *do* see we judge by our own standard. We conclude that a man who cries like a child on sight occasions, must always be incapable of acting or suffering with dignity; and that one who allows himself to be called a liar would not be ashamed of any baseness. Our writers also confound the distinctions of time and place; they combine in one character the Mahratta and the Bengalee; and tax the present generation with the crimes of the heroes of the Mahabharata. It might be argued, in opposition to many unfavourable testimonies, that those who have known the Indians longest have always the best opinion of them; but this is rather a compliment to human nature than to them, since it is true of every other people. It is more in point, that all persons who have retired from India think better of the people they have left, after comparing them with others, even of the most justly admired nations.'

But what is still more extraordinary than the ready acceptance of judgments unfavourable to the character of the Hindus, is the determined way in which public opinion, swayed by the statements of certain unfavourable critics, has persistently ignored the evidence which members of the Civil Service, officers and statesmen—men of the highest authority—have given again and again, in direct opposition to these unfavourable opinions. Here, too, I must ask to be allowed to quote at least a few of these witnesses on the other side.

Warren Hastings thus speaks of the Hindus in general: 'They are gentle and benevolent, more susceptible of gratitude for kindness shown them, and less prompted to vengeance for wrongs inflicted than any people on the face of the earth; faithful, affectionate, submissive to legal authority.'

Bishop Heber said: 'The Hindus are brave, courteous, intelligent, most eager for knowledge and improvement; sober, industrious, dutiful to parents, affectionate to their children, uniformly gentle and patient, and more easily affected by kindness and attention to their wants and feelings than any people I ever met with.'

Elphinstone states: 'No set of people among the Hindus are so depraved as the dregs of our own great towns. The villagers are everywhere amiable, affectionate to their families, kind to their neighbours, and, towards all but the government, honest and sincere. Including the Thugs and Dacoits, the mass of crime is less in India than in England. The Thugs are almost a separate nation, and the Dacoits are desperate ruffians in gangs. The Hindus are mild and gentle people, more merciful to prisoners than any other Asiatics. Their freedom from gross debauchery is the point in which they appear to most advantage; and their superiority in purity of manners is not flattering to our self-esteem.'

Yet Elphinstone can be most severe on the real faults of the people of India. He states that, at present, want of veracity is one of their prominent vices, but he adds 'that such deceit is most common in people connected with government, a class which spreads far in India, as, from the nature of the land-revenue, the lowest villager is often obliged to resist force by fraud.'

Sir John Malcolm writes: 'I have hardly ever known where a person did understand the language, or where a calm communication was made to a native of India, through a well-informed and trustworthy medium, that the result did not prove, that what had at first been stated as falsehood, had either proceeded from fear, or from misapprehension. I by no means wish to state that our Indian subjects are more free from this vice than other nations that occupy a nearly equal position in society, but I am positive that they are not more addicted to untruth.'

Sir Thomas Munro bears even stronger testimony. He writes: 'If a good system of agriculture, unrivalled manufacturing skill, a capacity to produce whatever can contribute to either convenience or luxury, schools established in every village for teaching, reading, writing, and arithmetic, the general practice of hospitality and charity amongst each other, and above all, a treatment of the female sex full of confidence, respect, and delicacy, are among the signs which denote a civilised people—than the Hindus are not inferior to the nations of Europe, and if civilisation is to become an article of trade between England and India, I am convinced that England will gain by the import cargo.'

My own experience with regard to the native character has been, of course, very limited. Those Hindus whom I have had the pleasure to know personally in Europe may be looked upon as exceptional, as the best specimens, it may be, that India could produce. Also, my intercourse with them has naturally been such that it could hardly have brought out the darker sides of human nature. During the last twenty years, however, I have had some excellent opportunities of watching a number of native scholars under circumstances where it is not difficult to detect a man's true character, I mean in literary work and, more particularly, in literary controversy. I have watched them carrying on such controversies both among themselves and with certain European scholars, and I feel bound to say that, with hardly one exception, they have displayed a far greater respect for truth, and a far more manly and generous spirit than we are accustomed to even in Europe and America. They have shown strength, but no rudeness; nay I know that nothing has surprised them so much as the coarse invective to which certain Sanskrit scholars have condescended, rudeness of speech being, according to their view of human nature, a safe sign not only of bad breeding, but of want of knowledge. When they were wrong, they have readily admitted their mistakes; when they were right, they have never sneered at their European adversaries. There has been, with few exceptions, no quibbling, no special pleading, no untruthfulness on their part, and certainly none of that low cunning of the scholar who writes down and publishes what he knows perfectly well to be false, and snaps his fingers at those who still value truth and self-respect more highly than victory or applause at any price. Here, too, we might possibly gain by the import cargo.

Let me add that I have been repeatedly told by English merchants that commercial honour stands higher in India than in any other country, and that a dishonoured bill is hardly known there.

I have left to the last the witnesses who might otherwise have been suspected—I mean the Hindus themselves. The whole of their literature from one end to other is pervaded by expressions of love and reverence for truth. Their very word for truth is full of meaning. It is *sat* or *satya, sat* being the participle of the verb *as,* to be. True, therefore, was with them simply *that which is.* The English *sooth* is connected with *sat,* also the Greek *on,* and the Latin *sens,* in *præsens.*

We are all very apt to consider truth to be what is trowed by others, or believed in by large majorities. That kind of truth is easy to accept. But whoever has once stood alone, surrounded by noisy assertions, and overwhelmed by the clamour of those who ought to know better, or perhaps, who did know better—call him Galileo or Darwin, Colenso or Stanley, or any other name—he knows what a real delight it is to feel in his heart of hearts, this is true—this is— this is *sat* — whatever daily, weekly, or quarterly papers, whatever bishops, archbishops, or popes, may say to the country.

Another name for truth is the Sanskrit *rita,* which originally seems to have meant *straight, direct,* while *anrita* is untrue, false.

Now one of the highest praises bestowed upon the gods in the Veda is that they are *satya,* true, truthful, trustworthy; and it is well known that both in modern and ancient times, men always ascribe to God or to their gods those qualities which they value most in themselves.

Other words applied to the gods as truthful beings, are *adrogha*, lit., not deceiving. *Adrogha-vak* means, he whose word is never broken. Thus Indra, the Vedic Jupiter, is said to have been praised by the fathers 'as reaching the enemy, overcoming him, standing on the summit, *true of speech*, most powerful in thought.'

Droghavak, on the contrary, is used for deceitful men. Thus Vasishtha, one of the great Vedic poets, says: 'If I had worshipped false gods, or if I believed in the gods vainly—but why art thou angry with us. O Jatavedas? May liars go to destruction!'

Satyam, as a neuter, is often used as an abstract, and is then rightly translated by truth. But it also means that which is, the true, the real; and there are several passages in the *Rigveda* where, instead of *truth*, I think we ought simply to translate *satyam* by the true, that is, the real, *to ontos on*. It sounds, no doubt, very well to translate *Satyena uttabhita bhumih* by 'the earth is founded on truth;' and I believe every translator has taken *satya* in that sense here. Ludwig translates, 'Von der Wahrheit ist die Erde gestützt.' But such an idea, if it conveys any tangible meaning at all, is far too abstract for those early poets and philosophers. They meant to say 'the earth, such as we see it, is held up, that is, rests on something real, though we may not see it, on something which they called the Real, and to which, in course of time, they gave many more names, such as *Rita*, the right, Brahman,' & c.

Of course where there is that strong reverence for truth, there must also be the sense of guilt arising from untruth. And thus we hear one poet pray that the waters may wash him clean, and carry off all his sins and all untruth:

'Carry away, ye waters, whatever evil there is in me, wherever I may have deceived, or may have cursed, and also all untruth (*anritam*).'

Or again, in the *Atharvaveda*, IV.16:

'May all thy fatal snares, which stand spread out seven by seven and threefold, catch the man who tells a lie, may they pass by him who tells the truth!'

From the Brahmanas, or theological treatises of the Brahmans, I shall quote a few passages only:

'Whosoever speaks the truth, makes the fire on his own altar blaze up, as if he poured butter into the lighted fire. His own light grows larger, and from tomorrow to tomorrow he becomes better. But whosoever speaks untruth, he quenches the fire on his altar, as if he poured water into the lighted fire; his own light grows smaller and smaller, and from tomorrow to tomorrow he becomes more wicked. Let man therefore speak truth only.'

And again: 'A man becomes impure by uttering falsehood.'

And again: 'As a man who steps on the edge of a sword placed over a pit cries out, I shall slip, I shall slip into the pit, so let a man guard himself from falsehood (or sin).'

In later times we see the respect for truth carried to such an extreme, that even a promise, unwittingly made, is considered to be binding.

In the *Katha Upanishad*, for instance, a father is introduced offering what is called an *All*-sacrifice, where everything is supposed to be given up. His son, who is standing by, taunts his father with not having altogether fulfilled his vow, because he has not sacrificed his son. Upon this, the father, though angry and against his will, is obliged to sacrifice his son. Again, when the son arrives in the lower world, he is allowed by the Judge of the Dead to ask for three favours. He then asks to be restored to life, to be taught some sacrificial mysteries, and, as the third boon, he asks to know what becomes of man after he is dead. Yama, the lord of the Departed, tries in vain to be let off from answering this last question. But he, too, is bound by his promise, and then follows a discourse on life after death, or immortal life, which forms one of the most beautiful chapter in the ancient literature of India.

The whole plot of one of the great Epic poems, the *Ramayana*, rests on a rash promise given by Dasaratha, king of Ayodhya, to his second wife, Kaikeyi, that he would grant her two boons. In order to secure the succession of her own son, she asks that Rama, the eldest son by the king's other wife, should be banished for fourteen years. Much as the king repents his promise, Rama, his eldest son, would on no account let his father break his word, and he leaves his kingdom to wander in the forest with his wife Sita and his brother Lakshmana. After the father's death, the son of the second wife declines the throne, and comes to Rama to persuade him to accept the kingdom of his father. But all in vain. Rama will keep his exile for fourteen years, and never disown his father's promise. Here follows a curious dialogue between a Brahman Jabali and Prince Rama, of which I shall give some extracts:

'The Brahman, who is a priest and courtier, says, "Well, descendant of Raghu, do not thou, so noble in sentiments, and austere in character, entertain, like a common man, this useless thought. What man is a kinsman of any other? What relationship has any one with another? A man is born alone and dies alone. Hence he who is attached to any one as his father or his mother, is to be regarded as if he were insane, for no one belongs to another. Thou oughtest not to abandon thy father's kingdom and stay here in a sad and miserable abode, attended with many trials. Let thyself be inaugurated king in the wealthy Ayodhya. Dasaratha, thy father is nothing to thee, or thou to him; the king is one, and thou another, do therefore what is said . . . . Then offer oblations to the departed spirits (of thy forefathers) on prescribed days; but see what a waste of food! For what can a dead man eat? If what is eaten by one here enters into the body of another (viz. of the departed), let Sraddhas be offered to those who are travelling; they need not then get food to eat on their journey. These books, the Vedas, (which enjoin men to sacrifice, give, consecrate themselves, practise austerities, and forsake the world), are composed by clever men to induce others to bestow gifts. Authoritative words do not fall from heaven. Let me, and others like yourselves, embrace whatever assertion is supported by reason. Adhere to what is apparent to the senses, and reject what is invisible . . . . *This world is the next world*; do thou therefore enjoy pleasure, for every virtuous man does not gain it. Virtuous men are greatly distressed, while the unrighteous are seen to be happy."'

These positivist sentiments sound strange, particularly from the mouth of a Brahman. But the poet evidently wishes to represent a Brahman living at court, who has an argument ready for anything and everything that is likely to please his king.

But what does Rama answer? 'The words,' he says, 'which you have addressed to me, though they recommend what *seems* to be right and salutary, advise, in fact, the contrary. The sinful transgressor, who lives according to the rules of heretical systems, obtains no esteem from good men. It is good conduct that marks a man to be noble or ignoble, heroic or a pretender to manliness, pure or impure. Truth and mercy are immemorial characteristics of a king's conduct. Hence royal rule is in its essence *truth*. On truth the world is based. Both sages and gods have esteemed truth. The man who speaks truth in this world attains the highest imperishable state. Men shrink with fear and horror from a liar as from a serpent. In this world the chief element in virtue is truth; it is called the basis of everything. Truth is lord in the world; virtue always rests on truth. All things are founded on truth; nothing is higher than it. Why, then, should I not be true to my promise, and faithfully observe the truthful injunction given by my father? Neither through covetousness, nor delusion, nor ignorance, will I, overpowered by darkness, break through the barrier of truth, but remain true to my promise to my father. How shall I, having promised to him that I would thus reside in the forest, transgress his injunction, and do what Bharata recommends?'

The other epic poem too, the *Mahabharata*, is full of episodes showing a profound regard for truth and an almost slavish submission to a pledge once given. The death of Bhishma, one of the most important events in the story of the *Mahabharata*, is due to his vow never to hurt a woman. He is thus killed by Sikhandin, whom he takes to be a woman.

Were I to quote from all the law-books, and from still later works, everywhere you would hear the same keynote of truthfulness vibrating through them all.

We must not, however, suppress the fact that, under certain circumstances, a lie was allowed, or, at all events, excused by Indian lawgivers. Thus Gautama says: 'An untruth spoken by people under the influence of anger, excessive joy, fear, pain, or grief, by infants, by very old men, by persons labouring under a delusion, being under the influence of drink, or by mad men, does not cause the speaker to fall or, as we should say, is a venial, nor a mortal sin.'

This is a large admission, yet even in that open admission there is a certain amount of honesty. Again and again in the *Mahabharata* is this excuse pleaded. Nay there is in the *Mahabharata* the well-known story of Kausika, called Satyavadin, the Truth-speaker, who goes to hell for having spoken the truth. He once saw men flying into the forest before robbers (*dasyu*). The robbers came up soon after them, and asked Kausika, which way the fugitives had taken. He told them the truth, and the men were caught by the robbers and killed. But Kausika, we are told, went to hell for having spoken the truth.

The Hindus may seem to have been a priest-ridden race, and their devotion to sacrifice and ceremonial is well known. Yet this is what the poet of the *Mahabharata* dares of say:

'Let a thousand sacrifices (of a horse) and truth be weighed in the balance—truth will exceed the thousand sacrifices.'

These are words addressed by Sakuntala, the deserted wife, to King Dushyanta, when he declined to recognise her and his son. And when he refuses to listen to her appeal, what does she appeal to as the highest authority?—*The voice of conscience.*

'If you think I am alone,' she says to the king, 'you do not know that wise man within your heart. He knows of your evil deed—in *his* sight you commit sin. A man who has committed sin may think that no one knows it. The gods know it and the old man within.'

This must suffice. I say once more that I do not wish to represent the people of India as so many millions of angels, but I do wish it to be understood and to be accepted as a fact, that the damaging charge of untruthfulness brought against that people is utterly unfounded with regard to ancient times. It is not only not true, but the very opposite of the truth. As to modern times, and I date them from about 1,000 after Christ, I can only say this. If you frighten a child, that child will tell a lie—if you terrorise millions, you must not be surprised if they try to escape from your fangs. Truthfulness is a luxury, perhaps the greatest, and let me assure you, the most expensive in our life—and happy the man who has been able to enjoy it from his very childhood. It may be easy enough in our days and in a free country, like England, never to tell a lie—but the older we grow, the harder we find it to be always true, to speak the truth, the whole truth and nothing but the truth. The Hindus too had made that discovery. They too knew how hard, nay how impossible it is, always to speak the truth, the whole truth, and nothing but the truth. There is a short story in the *Satapatha Brahmana,* to my mind full of deep meaning, and pervaded by the real sense of truth, the real sense of the difficulty of truth. His kinsman said to Aruna Aupavesi, 'Thou art advanced in years, establish thou the sacrificial fires.' He replied: 'Thereby you tell me henceforth to keep silence. For he who has established the fires must not speak an untruth, and only by not speaking at all, one speaks no untruth. To that extent the service of the sacrificial fires consists in truth.'

I doubt whether in any other of the ancient literatures of the world you will find traces of that extreme sensitiveness of conscience which despairs of our ever speaking the truth, and which declares silence gold, and speech silver, though in a much higher sense than our proverb.

What I should wish to impress on those who will soon find themselves the rulers of millions of human beings in India, is the duty to shake off national prejudices, which are apt to degenerate into a kind of madness. I have known people with a brown skin whom I could look up to as my betters. Look for them in India, and you will find them, and if you meet with disappointments, as, no doubt you will, think of the people with white skins whom you have trusted, and whom you can trust no more. We are all apt to be Pharisees in international judgments. I read only a few days ago in a pamphlet written by an enlightened politician, the following words:

'Experience only can teach that nothing is so truly astonishing to a morally depraved people as the phenomenon of a race of men in whose word perfect confidence may be placed . . . . The natives are conscious of their inferiority in nothing so much as in this. They require to be taught rectitude of conduct much more than literature and science.'

It you approach the Hindus with such feelings, you will teach them neither rectitude, nor science, nor literature. Nay, they might appeal to their own literature, even to their law-books, to teach us at least one lesson of truthfulness, truthfulness to ourselves, or, in other words,—humility.

What does Yajnavalkya say?

'It is not our hermitage,' he says—our religion we might say—'still less the colour of our skin, that produces virtue; virtue must be practised. Therefore let no one do to others what he would not have done to himself.'

And the Laws of the Manavas, which were so much abused by Mill, what do they teach?

'Evil doers think indeed that no one sees them; but the gods see them, and the old man within.'

'Self is the witness of Self, Self is the refuge of Self. Do not despise thy own Self, the highest witness of men.'

'If, friend, thou thinkest thou art self-alone, remember there is the silent thinker (the Highest Self) always within thy heart, and *he* sees what is good, and what is evil.'

'O friend, whatever good thou mayest have done from thy very birth, all will go to the dogs, if thou speak an untruth.'

Or in Vasishtha:

'Practise righteousness, not unrighteousness; speak truth, not untruth; look far, not near; look up towards the Highest, not towards anything low.'

No doubt, there is moral depravity in India, and where is there no moral depravity in this world? But to appeal to international statistics would be, I believe, a dangerous game. Nor must we forget that our standards of morality differ, and, on some points, differ considerably from those recognised in India; and we must not wonder, if sons do not at once condemn as criminal what their fathers and grandfathers considered right. Let us hold by all means to *our* sense of what is right and what is wrong; but in judging others, whether in public or in private life, whether as historians or politicians, let us not forget that a kindly spirit will never do any harm. Certainly I can imagine nothing more mischievous, more dangerous, more fatal to the permanence of English rule in India, than for the young Civil Servants to go to that country with the idea that it is a sink of moral depravity, an ant's nest of lies; for no one is so sure to go wrong, whether in public or in private life, as he who says in his haste: 'All men are liars.'

Notes

Pages

25. **Sir John Malcolm** (1769-1833): Distinguished himself in the E.I. Company's military and diplomatic service. Author of *A History of Persia* and several works on Indian historical subjects.

26. **Wilson** (Horace Hayman, 1786-1860): Was in the E.I. Company's service in India from 1808-32. Assay-master of the Calcutta mint, 1816-32. A great orientalist who combined a variety of attainments as linguist, historian, chemist, accountant, numismatist, actor and musician. An edition of the *Vishnu Purana*, a translation of the *Rigveda* and the edition with a continuation of Mill's *History of India* are the best known among his works.

28. **Keshub Chunder Sen** (1838-84) : Founder of the Brahmo Samaj of India which was started in 1866 as distinct from the original Brahmo Samaj founded by Raja Ram Mohan Roy in 1828. Thrown much into the society of Christian missionaries, Sen exerted himself to reform Indian society along lines suggested by them.

    Another Professor of Sanskrit: E.B. Cowell (1826-1903). First Professor of Sanskrit at Cambridge, 1867. Professor of History and Political Economy, Presidency College, Calcutta (1856-64). Also Principal of the Sanskrit College, Calcutta, from 1858-64, when he left India.

    Col. Sleeman (1788-1856) : Soldier, diplomat, author. Advised against the annexation of Oudh.

    Mill (James): Published in 1818 his *History of British India*. Associate of Bentham and Ricardo and father of John Stuart Mill.

29. **Dr. Robertson** (William, 1721-93): Scottish historian; author of *Disquisition Concerning the Knowledge which the Ancients had of India* (1791).

31. **Sir Henry Maine** (1822-88): Legal member of the Supreme Council of India from 1862-69. Professor of Jurisprudence at Oxford, 1869-78. Author of *Ancient Law* (1861), *Village Communities in the East* and *West* (1871) and other works.

    Megasthenes: Greek ambassador in Chandragupta Maurya's Court at Pataliputra, 4th century BC.

32. **Nearchus:** Greek Admiral who came to India with Alexander the Great, some years before Megasthenes.

35. **Artaxerxes Mnemon:** King of Persia, 405-359 BC. Defeated and killed at the battle of Cunaxa by his brother Cyrus who had rebelled against him.
38. **Mountstuart Elphinstone** (1779-1859): Governor of Bombay, 1819-27; twice refused the Governor-Generalship of India. The Elphinstone College, Bombay, was founded in his honour. His *History of India* (1841) has earned for him the title of 'The Tacitus of Modern Historians.'
39. **Bishop Heber** (1783-1826): Bishop of Calcutta; travelled continuously throughout India in the discharge of his episcopal duties, and wrote a narrative of his travels in his *Journey through India.* Died at Trichinopoly.
41. **Galileo** (Galiei, 1564-1642): Italian mathematician and physicist. Persecuted by the Inquisition for his opinion that the sun, not the earth, was the centre of the planetary world. He was the founder of experimental science in Italy.
    Darwin (Charles,1809-82): His *Origin of the Species,* published in 1859, started the theory of Evolution, which was at first violently opposed.
    Colenso (J.W., 1814-83): Bishop of Natal. His criticisms of certain books of the *Bible* led to his excommunication; he was, however, restored to his see by the law courts.
    Stanley (Aurther, 1815-81): Dean of Westminster. Leader of the Broad Church Movement and courageous advocate of religious toleration.
42. **Yon der Wahrheit etc.:** 'By the truth is the earth supported.'
43. **His son:** called Nachiketas.
45. **Bhishma:** Son of Santanu and Ganga; in the great war he took the side of the Kauravas against the Pandavas; he was renowned for his continence, wisdom, bravery and fidelity to his word. (Monier-Williams).
    Sikhandin: Born as a women, but changed to a male by a Yaksha.

LECTURE III

Human Interest of Sanskrit Literature

MY first Lecture was intended to remove the prejudice that India is and always must be a strange country to us, and that those who have to live there will find themselves stranded, and far away from that living stream of thoughts and interests which carries us along in England and in other countries of Europe.

My second Lecture was directed against another prejudice, namely, that the people of India with whom the young Civil Servants will have to pass the best years of their life are a race so depraved morally, and more particularly so devoid of any regard for truth, that they *must* always remain strangers to us, and that any real fellowship or friendship with them is quite out of the question.

Today I shall have to grapple with a third prejudice, namely, that the literature of India, and more especially the classical Sanskrit literature, whatever may be its interest to the scholar and the antiquarian, has little to teach us which we cannot learn better from other sources, and that at all events it is of little practical use to young civilians. If only they learn to express themselves in Hindustani or Tamil, that is considered quite enough; nay, as they have to deal with men and with the ordinary affairs of life, and as, before everything else, they are to be men of the world and men of business, it is even supposed to be dangerous, if they allowed themselves to become absorbed in questions of abstruse scholarship or in researches on ancient religion, mythology, and philosophy.

I take the very opposite opinion, and I should advise every young man who wishes to enjoy his life in India, and to spend his years there with profit to himself and to others, to learn Sanskrit, and to learn it well.

I know it will be said, what can be the use of Sanskrit at the present day? Is not Sanskrit a dead language? And are not the Hindus themselves ashamed of their ancient literature? Do they not learn English, and do they not prefer Locke, and Hume, and Mill to their ancient poets and philosophers?

No doubt Sanskrit, in one sense, is a dead language. It was, I believe, a dead language more than two thousand years ago. Buddha, about 500 BC, commanded his disciples to preach in the dialects of the people; and King Asoka, in the third century BC, when he put up his Edicts, which were intended to be read or, at least, to be understood by the people, had them engraved on rocks and pillars in the various local dialects from Cabul in the North to Mysore in the South, from Gujerat in the West to Orissa in the East. These various dialects are as different from Sanskrit as Italian is from Latin, and we have therefore good reason to suppose that, in the third century BC, if not earlier, Sanskrit had ceased to be the spoken language of the people at large.

There is an interesting passage in the *Chullavagga*, where we are told that, even during Buddha's lifetime, some of his pupils, who were Brahmans by birth, complained that people spoiled the words of Buddha by every one repeating them in his own dialect (*nirukti*). They proposed to translate his words into Sanskrit; but he declined, and commanded that each man should learn his doctrine in his own language.

And there is another passage, quoted by Hardy in his *Manual of Buddhism*, where we read that at the time of Buddha's first preaching each of the countless listeners thought that the sage was looking towards him, and was speaking to him in his own tongue, though the language used was Magadhi.

Sanskrit, therefore, as a language spoken by the people at large, had ceased to exist in the third century BC.

Yet such is the marvellous continuity between the past and the present in India, that in spite of repeated social convulsions, religious reforms, and foreign invasions, Sanskrit may be said to be still the only language that is spoken over the whole extent of that vast country.

Though the Buddhist sovereigns published their edicts in the vernaculars, public inscriptions and private official documents are composed in Sanskrit to the present day. And though the language of the sacred writings of Buddhists and Jainas was borrowed from the vulgar dialects, the literature of India never ceased to be written in Paninean Sanskrit, while the few exceptions, as, for instance, the use of Prakrit by women and inferior characters in the plays of Kalidasa and others, are themselves not without an important historical significance.

Even at the present moment, after a century of English rule and English teaching, I believe that Sanskrit is more widely understood in India than Latin was in Europe at the time of Dante.

Whenever I receive a letter from a learned man in India, it is written in Sanskrit. Whenever there is a controversy on questions of law and religion, the pamphlets published in India are written in Sanskrit. There are journals written in Sanskrit which must entirely depend for their support on readers who prefer that classical language to the vulgar dialects. There is *The Pandit*, published at Benares, containing not only editions of ancient texts, but treatises on modern subjects, reviews of books published in England, and controversial articles, all in Sanskrit.

Another paper of the same kind is the *Pratna-Kamra-nandini*, 'the Delight of lovers of old things,' published likewise at Benares, and full of valuable materials.

There is also the *Vidyodaya*, 'the Rise of Knowledge,' a Sanskrit journal published at Calcutta, which sometimes contains important articles. There are probably others, which I do not know.

There is a monthly serial published at Bombay, by M. Moreshwar Kunte, called the *Shad-darshana-chintanika*, or 'Studies in Indian Philosophy,' giving the text of the ancient systems of philosophy, with commentaries and treatises, written in Sanskrit, though in this case accompanied by a Marathi and an English translation.

Of the *Rigveda*, the most ancient of Sanskrit books, two editions are now coming out in monthly numbers, the one published at Bombay, by what may be called the liberal party, the other at Prayaga (Allahabad) by Dayananda Sarasvati, the representative of Indian orthodoxy. The former gives a paraphrase in Sanskrit, and a Marathi and an English translation; the latter a full explanation in Sanskrit, followed by a vernacular commentary. These books are published by subscription, and the list of subscribers among the natives of India is very considerable.

There are other journals, which are chiefly written in the spoken dialects, such as Bengali, Marathi, or Hindi; but they contain occasional articles in Sanskrit also, as, for instance, the *Harischandrachan-*

drika, published at Benares, the *Tattvabodhini*, published at Calcutta, and several more.

It was only the other day that I saw in the *Liberal*, the journal of Keshub Chunder Sen's party, an account of a meeting between Brahmavrata Samadhyayi, a Vedic scholar of Nuddea, and Kashinath Trimbak Telang, a M.A. of the University of Bombay. The one came from the east, the other from the west, yet both could converse fluently in Sanskrit.

Still more extraordinary is the number of Sanskrit texts, issuing from native presses, for which there seems to be a large demand, for if we write for copies to be sent to England, we often find that, after a year or two, all the copies have been bought up in India itself. That would not be the case with Anglo-Saxon texts in England, or with Latin texts in Italy!

But more than this, we are told that the ancient epic poems of the *Mahabharata* and *Ramayana* are still recited in the temples for the benefit of visitors, and that in the villages large crowds assemble around the *Kathaka*, the reader of these ancient Sanskrit poems, often interrupting his recitations with tears and sighs, when the hero of the poem is sent into banishment, while when he returns to his kingdom, the houses of the village are adorned with lamps and garlands. Such a recitation of the whole of the *Mahabharata* is said to occupy ninety days, or sometimes half a year. The people at large require, no doubt, that the Brahman narrator (*Kathaka*) should interpret the old poem, but there must be some few people present who understand, or imagine they understand, the old poetry of Vyasa and Valmiki.

There are numbers of Brahmans even now, when so little inducement exists for Vedic studies, who know the whole of the *Rigveda* by heart and can repeat it; and what applies to the *Rigveda* applies to many other books.

But even if Sanskrit were more of a dead language than it really is, all the living languages of India, both Aryan and Dravidian draw their very life and soul from Sanskrit. On this point, and on the great help that even a limited knowledge of Sanskrit would render in the acquisition of the vernaculars, I, and others better qualified than I am, have spoken so often, though without any practical effect, that I need not speak again. Any candidate who knows but the elements of Sanskrit grammar will well understand what I mean, whether his special vernacular may be Bengali, Hindustani, or even Tamil. To a classical scholar I can only say that between a Civil Servant who knows Sanskrit and Hindustani, and another who knows Hindustani only, there is about the same difference in their power of forming an intelligent appreciation of India and its inhabitants, as there is between a traveller who visits, Italy with a knowledge of Latin, and a party personally conducted to Rome by Messrs Cook and Co.

Let us examine, however, the objection that Sanskrit literature is a dead or an artificial literature, a little more carefully, in order to see whether there is not some kind of truth in it. Some people hold that the literary works which we possess in Sanskrit never had any real life at all, that they were altogether scholastic productions, and that therefore they can teach us nothing of what we really care for, namely the historical growth of the Hindu mind. Others maintain that at the present moment, at all events, and after a century of English rule, Sanskrit literature has ceased to be a motive power in India, and that it can teach us nothing of what is passing now through the Hindu mind and influencing it for good or for evil.

Let us look at the facts. Sanskrit literature is a wide and a vague term. It the Vedas, such as we now have them, were composed about 1500 BC, and if it is a fact that considerable works continue to be written in Sanskrit even now, we have before us a stream of literary activity extending over three thousand four hundred years. With the exception of China there is nothing like this in the whole world.

It is difficult to give an idea of the enormous extent and variety of that literature. We are only gradually becoming acquainted with the untold treasures which still exist in manuscripts, and with the titles of that still larger number of works which must have existed formerly, some of them being still quoted by writers of the last three or four centuries.

The Indian Government has of late years ordered a kind of bibliographical survey of India to be made, and has sent some learned Sanskrit scholars, both European and native, to place where collections of Sanskrit MSS are known to exist, in order to examine and catalogue them. Some of these catalogues have been published, and we learn from them that the number of separate works in Sanskrit, of which MSS are still in existence, amounts to about 10,000. This is more, I believe, than the whole classical literature of Greece and Italy put together. Much of it no doubt; will be called mere rubbish; but then you know that even in our days the writings of a very eminent philosopher have been called 'mere rubbish.'

What I wish you to see is this, that there runs through the whole history of India, through its three of four thousand years, a high road, or, it is perhaps more accurate to say, a high mountain-path of literature. It may be remote from the turmoil of the plain, hardly visible perhaps to the millions of human beings in their daily struggle of life. It may have been trodden by a few solitary wanderers only. But to the historian of the human race, to the student of the development of the human mind, those few solitary wanderers are after all the true representatives of India from age to age. Do not let us be deceived. The true history of the world must always be the history of the few; and as we measure the Himalaya by the height of Mount Everest, we must take the true measure of India from the poets of the Veda, the sages of the Upanishads, the founders of the Vedanta and Sankhya philosophies, and the authors of the oldest law-books, and not from the millions who are born and die in their villages, and who have never for one moment been roused out of their drowsy dream of life.

To large multitudes in India, no doubt, Sanskrit literature was not merely a dead literature, it was simply non-existent; but the same might be said of almost every literature, and more particularly of the literatures of the ancient world.

Still, with all this, I am quite prepared to acknowledge to a certain extent the truth of the statement, that a great portion of Sanskrit literature has never been living and national, in the same sense in which the Greek and Roman literatures reflected at times the life of a whole nation; and it is quite true besides, that the Sanskrit books which are best known to the public at large, belong to what might correctly be called the Renaissance period of Indian literature, when those who wrote Sanskrit had themselves to learn the language, as we learn Latin, and were conscious that they were writing for a learned and cultivated public only, and not for the people at large.

This will require a fuller explanation.

We may divide the whole of Sanskrit literature beginning with the *Rigveda* and ending with Dayananda's Introduction to his edition of the *Rigveda*, his by no means uninteresting *Rigveda-bhumika*, into two great periods: that preceding the great Turanian invasion, and that following it.

The former comprises the Vedic literature and the ancient literature of Buddhism, the latter all the rest.

If I call the invasion which is generally called the invasion of the

Sakas, or the Scythians, or Indo-Scythians, or Turushkas, the Turanian invasion, it is simply because I do not as yet wish to commit myself more than I can help as to the nationality of the tribes who took possession of India, or, at least, of the government of India, from about the first century BC to the third century AD.

They are best known by the name of Yueh-chi, this being the name by which they are called in Chinese chronicles. These Chinese chronicles from the principal source from which we derive our knowledge of these tribes, both before and after their invasion of India. Many theories have been started as to their relationship with other races. They are described as of pink and white complexion and as shooting from horseback; and as there was some similarity between their Chinese name Yueh-chi and the Gothi or Goths, they were identified by Remusat with those German tribes, and by others with the Getae, the neighbours of the Goths. Tod went even a step further, and traced the Jats in India and the Rajputs back to the Yueh-chi and Getae. Some light may come in time out of all this darkness, but for the present we must be satisfied with the fact that, between the first century before and the third century after our era, the greatest political revolution took place in India owing to the repeated inroads of Turanian, or, to use a still less objectionable term, of Northern tribes. Their presence in India, recorded by Chinese historians, is fully confirmed by coins, by inscriptions, and by the traditional history of the country, such as it is; but to my mind nothing attests the presence of these foreign invaders more clearly than the break, or, I could almost say, the blank in the Brahmanical literature of India from the first century before to the third century after our era.

If we consider the political and social state of that country, we can easily understand what would happen in a case of invasion and conquest by a warlike race. The invaders would take possession of the strongholds or castles, and either remove the old Rajahs, or make them their vassals and agents. Everything else would then go on exactly as before. The rents would be paid, the taxes collected, and the life of the villagers, that is, of the great majority of the people of India, would go on almost undisturbed by the change of government. The only people who might suffer would be, or, at all events, might be the priestly caste, unless they should come to terms with the new conquerors. The priestly caste, however, was also to a great extent the literary caste, and the absence of their old patrons, the native Rajahs, might well produce for a time a complete cessation of literary activity. The rise of Buddhism and its formal adoption by King Asoka had already considerably shaken the power and influence of the old Brahmanic hierarchy. The Northern conquerors, whatever their religion may have been, were certainly not believers in the Veda. They seem to have made a kind of compromise with Buddhism, and it is probably due to that compromise, or to an amalgamation of Saka legends with Buddhist doctrines, that we owe the so-called Mahayana form of Buddhism which was finally settled at the Council under Kanishka, one of the Turanian rulers of India in the first century AD.

If then we divide the whole of Sanskrit literature into these two periods, the one anterior to the great Turanian invasion, the other posterior to it, we may call the literature of the former period *ancient* and *natural*, that of the latter *modern* and *artificial*.

Of the former period we possess, *first*, what has been called the Veda, i.e., knowledge, in the widest sense of the word—a considerable mass of literature, yet evidently a wreck only, saved out of a general deluge; *secondly*, the works collected in the Buddhist *Tripitaka*, now known to us chiefly in what is called the Pali dialect, the Gatha dialects, and Sanskrit, and probably much added to in later times.

The second period of Sanskrit literature comprehends everything else. Both periods may be subdivided again, but this does not concern us at present.

Now I am quite willing to admit that the literature of the second period, the modern Sanskrit literature, never was a living or national literature. It may here and there contain relics of earlier times, adapted to the literary, religious, and moral tastes of a later period; and whenever we are able to disentangle those ancient elements, they may serve to throw light on the past, and, to a certain extent, supplement what has been lost in the literature of the Vedic times. The metrical Law-books, for instance, contain old materials which existed during the Vedic period, partly in prose, as Sutras, partly in more ancient metres, as Gathas. The Epic poems, the *Mahabharata* and *Ramayana*, have taken the place of the old Itihasas and Akhyanas. The Puranas, even, may contain materials, though much altered, of what was called in Vedic literature the Purana.

But the great mass of that later literature is artificial or scholastic, full of interesting compositions, and by no means devoid of originality and occasional beauty; yet, with all that, curious only, and appealing to the interests of the Oriental scholar far more than the broad human sympathies of the historian and the philosopher.

It is different with the ancient literature of India, the literature dominated by the Vedic and the Buddhistic religions. That literature opens to us a chapter in what has been called the Education of the Human Race, to which we can find no parallel anywhere else. Whoever cares for the historical growth of our language, that is, of our thoughts; whoever cares for the first intelligible development of religion and mythology; whoever cares for the first foundation of what in later times we call the sciences of astronomy, metronomy, grammar, and etymology; whoever cares for the first intimations of philosophical thought, for the first attempts at regulating family life, village life, and state life, as founded on religion, ceremonial, tradition and contract (*samaya*)—must in future pay the same attention to the literature of the Vedic period as to the literatures of Greece and Rome and Germany.

As to the lessons which the early literature of Buddhism may teach us, I need not dwell on them at present. If I may judge from the numerous questions that are addressed to me with regard to that religion and its striking coincidences with Christianity, Buddhism has already become a subject of general interest, and will and ought to become so more and more. On that whole class of literature, however, it is not my intention to dwell in this short course of Lectures, which can hardly suffice even for a general survey of Vedic literature, and for an elucidation of the principal lessons which, I think, we may learn from the Hymns, the Brahmanas, the Upanishads, and the Sutras.

It was a real misfortune that Sanskrit literature became first known to the learned public in Europe through specimens belonging to the second, or, what I called, the Renaissance period. The *Bhagavadgita*, the plays of Kalidasa, such as *Sakuntala* or *Urvasi*, a few episodes from the *Mahabharata* and *Ramayana*, such as that of Nala, the fables of the *Hitopadesa*, and the sentences of Bhartrihari are, no doubt, extremely curious; and as, at the time when they first became known in Europe, they were represented to be of extreme antiquity, and the work of a people formerly supposed to be quite incapable of high literary efforts, they naturally attracted the attention of men such as Sir William Jones in England, Herder and Goethe in Germany, who were pleased to speak of them in terms of highest admiration. It was the fashion at that time to speak of Kalidasa, as, for instance, Alexander von Humboldt did even in so recent a work as his *Kosmos*, as 'the great contemporary of Virgil and Horace, who lived at the splendid Court of Vikramaditya,' this Vikramaditya being supposed to be the founder of the Samvat era, 56 BC. But all this is now changed. Whoever the Vikramaditya was who is supposed to have defeated the Sakas, and to have founded another era, the Samvat era, 56 BC, he certainly did not live in the first century BC. Nor are the Indians looked upon any longer as an illiterate race, and their poetry as popular and artless. On the contrary, they are judged now by the same standards as Persians and Arabs, Italians or French; and, measured by that standard, such works as Kalidasa's plays are not superior to many plays that have long been allowed to rest in dust and peace on the shelves of our libraries. Their antiquity is no longer believed in by any critical Sanskrit scholar. Kalidasa is mentioned with Bharavi as a famous poet in an inscription dated AD 585-6 (507 Saka era), and for the present I see no reason to place him much earlier. Avinita, who wrote a commentary on fifteen cantos of Bharavi's *Kiratarjuniya*, is said to have lived about AD 470. But even if we accept this date, Bharavi and Kalidasa need not have lived before the fifth or fourth century AD. As to the Laws of Manu, which used to be assigned to a fabulous antiquity, and are so still sometimes by those who write at random or at second-hand, I doubt whether, in their present form they can be older than the fourth century of our era, nay I am quite prepared to see an ever later date assigned to them. I know this will seem heresy to many Sanskrit scholars, but we must try to be honest to ourselves. Is there any evidence to constrain us to assign the *Manavadharmasastra*, such as we now possess it, written in continuous *slokas*, to any date anterior to AD 300 ? And if there is not, why should we not openly state it, challenge opposition, and feel grateful if our doubts can be removed?

That Manu was a name of high legal authority before that time, and that Manu and the Manavam are frequently quoted in the ancient legal Sutras, is quite true; but this serves only to confirm the conviction that the literature which succeeded the Turanian invasion is full of wrecks saved from the intervening deluge. If what we call the Laws of Manu had really existed as a Code of Laws, like the Code of Justinian, during previous centuries, is it likely that it should nowhere have been quoted and appealed to?

Varahamihira (who died AD 587) refers to Manu several times, but not to a *Manavadharmasastra*; and the only time where he seems actually to quote a number of verses from Manu, these verses are not to be met with in our text.

I believe it will be found that the fourth, fifth, and sixth centuries were the age of the literary Renaissance in India. That Kalidasa and Bharavi were famous at that time, we know from the evidence of inscriptions. We know that in the sixth century the fame of Indian literature had reached Persia, and that the King of Persia, Khosru Nushirvan (reigned AD 531-79), sent his physician, Barzoi, to India, in order to translate the fables of the *Panchatantra*, or rather their original, from Sanskrit into Pahlavi. The famous 'Nine Gems,' or 'the nine classics,' as we should say, have been referred, at least in part, to the same age, and I doubt whether we shall be able to assign a much earlier date to anything we possess of Sanskrit literature, excepting always the Vedic and Buddhistic writings.

Although the specimens of this modern Sanskrit literature, when they first became known, served to arouse a general interest, and serve even now to keep alive a certain superficial sympathy for Indian literature, more serious students had soon disposed of these compositions, and while gladly admitting their claim to be called pretty and attractive, could not think of allowing to Sanskrit literature a place among the world-literatures, a place by the side of Greek and Latin, Italian, French, English or German.

There was indeed a time when people began to imagine that all that was worth knowing about Indian literature was known, and that the only ground on which Sanskrit could claim a place among the recognised branches of learning in a University was its usefulness for the study of the Science of Language.

At that very time, however, now about forty years ago, a new start was made, which has given to Sanskrit scholarship an entirely new character. The chief author of that movement was Burnouf, then Professor at the College de France in Paris, an excellent scholars, but at the same time a man of wide views and true historical instincts, and the last man to waste his life on mere Nalas and Sakuntalas. Being brought up in the old traditions of the classical school in France (his father was the author of the well-known Greek grammar), then for a time a promising young barrister, with influential friends such as Guizot, Thiers, Mignet, Villemain, at his side, and with a brilliant future before him, he was not likely to spend his life on pretty Sanskrit ditties. What he wanted when he threw himself on Sanskrit was history, human history, world-history, and with an unerring grasp he laid hold of Vedic literature and Buddhist literature, as the two stepping-stones in the slough of Indian literature. He died young, and has left a few arches only of the building he wished to rear. But his spirit lived on in his pupils and his friends, and few would deny that the first impulse, directly or indirectly, to all that has been accomplished since by the students of Vedic and Buddhist literature, was given by Burnouf and his lectures at the College de France.

What then, you may ask, do we find in that ancient Sanskrit literature and cannot find anywhere else? My answer is, we find there the Aryan man, whom we know in his various characters, as Greek, Roman, German, Celt, and Slav, in an entirely new character. Whereas in his migrations northward his active and political energies are called out and brought to their highest perfection, we find the other side of the human character, the passive and meditative, carried to its fullest growth in India. In some of the hymns of the *Rig-veda* we can still watch an earlier phase. We see the Aryan tribes taking possession of the land, and under the guidance of such warlike gods as Indra and the Maruts, defending their new homes against the assaults of the black-skinned aborigines as well as against the inroads of later Aryan colonists. But that period of war soon came to an end, and when the great mass of the people had once settled down in their homesteads, the military and political duties seem to have been monopolised by what we call a *caste*, that is by a small aristocracy, while the great majority of the people were satisfied with spending their days within the narrow spheres of their villages, little concerned about the outside world, and content with the gifts that nature bestowed on them without much labour. Bhartrihari says:

'There is fruit on the trees in every forest, which every one who likes may pluck without trouble. There is cool and sweet water in the pure rivers here and there. There is a soft bed made of the twigs of beautiful creepers. And yet wretched people suffer pain at the door of the rich!'

At first sight we may feel inclined to call this quiet enjoyment of life, this mere looking on, a degeneracy rather than a growth. It seems so different from what *we* think life ought to be. Yet, from a higher point of view, it may appear that those Southern Aryas have chosen the good part, or at least the part good for them, while we, Northern Aryas, have been careful and troubled about many things.

It is at all events a problem worth considering whether, as there is in nature a South and a North, there are not two hemispheres also in human nature, both worth developing—the active, combative, and political on the side, the passive, meditative, and philosophical on the other; and for the solution of that problem no literature furnishes such ample materials as that of the Veda, beginning with the hymns and ending with the Upanishads. We enter into a new world—not always an attractive one, least of all to us; but it possesses one charm, it is real, it is of natural growth and like everything of natural growth, I believe it had a hidden purpose, and was intended to teach us some kind of lesson that is worth learning and that certainly we could learn nowhere else. We are not called upon either to admire or to despise that ancient Vedic literature; we have simply to study and to try to understand it.

There have been silly persons who have represented the development of the Indian mind as superior to any other, nay, who would make us go back to the Veda or to the sacred writings of the Buddhists in order to find there a truer religion, a purer morality, and a more sublime philosophy than our own. I shall not even mention the names of these writers or the titles of their works. But I feel equally impatient when I see other scholars criticising the ancient literature of India as if it were the work of the nineteenth century, as if it represented an enemy that must be defeated, and that can claim no mercy at our hands. That the Veda is full of childish, silly, even to our minds monstrous conceptions, who would deny? But even these monstrosities are interesting and instructive; nay, many of them, if we can but make allowance for different ways of thought and language, contain germs of truth and rays of light, all the more striking, because breaking upon as through the veil of the darkest night.

Here lies the general, the truly human interest which are *ancient* literature of India possesses, and which gives it a claim on the attention, not only of Oriental scholars or of students of ancient history, but of every educated man and woman.

There are problems which we may put aside for a time, aye, which we must put aside while engaged each in our own hard struggle for life, but which will recur for all that, and which, whenever they do recur, will stir us more deeply than we like to confess to others, or even to ourselves. It is true that with us one day only out of seven is set apart for rest and meditation, and for the consideration of what the Greeks called *ta megista*—'the greatest things.' It is true that that seventh day also is passed by many of us either in mere church-going routine or in thoughtless rest. But whether on week-days or on

Sundays, whether in youth or in old age, there are moments, rare though they be, yet for all that the most critical moments of our life, when the old simple questions of humanity return to us in all their intensity, and we ask ourselves, What are we? What is this life on earth meant for? Are we to have no rest here, but to be always toiling and building up our own happiness out of the ruins of the happiness of our neighbours? And when we have made our home on earth as comfortable as it can be made with steam and gas and electricity, are we really so much happier than the Hindu in his primitive homestead?

With us, as I said just now, in these Northern climates, where life is and always must be a struggle, and a hard struggle too, and where accumulation of wealth has become almost a necessity to guard against the uncertainties of old age or the accidents inevitable in our complicated social life, with us, I say, and in our society, hours of rest and meditation are but few and far between. It was the same as long as we know the history of the Teutonic races; it was the same even with Romans and Greeks. The European climate with its long cold winters, in many places also the difficulty of cultivating the soil, the conflict of interests between small communities, has developed the instinct of self-preservation (not to say, self-indulgence) to such an extent that most of the virtues and most of the vices of European society can be traced back to that source. Our own character was formed under these influences, by inheritance, by education, by necessity. We all lead a fighting-life; our highest ideal of life is a fighting-life. We work till we can work no longer, and are proud, like old horses, to die in harness. We point with inward satisfaction to what we and our ancestors have achieved by hard work, in founding a family or a business, a town or a state. We point to the marvels of what we call civilization—our splendid cities, our high-roads and bridges, our ships, our railways, our telegraphs, our electric light, our pictures, our statues, our music, our theatres. We imagine we have made life on earth quite perfect; in some cases so perfect that we are almost sorry to leave it again. But the lesson which both Brāhmans and Buddhists are never tired of teaching is that this life is but a journey from one village to another, and not a resting-place. Thus we read:

'As a man journeying to another village may enjoy a night's rest in the open air, but, after leaving his resting-place, proceeds again on his journey the next day, thus father, mother, wife, and wealth are all but like a night's rest to us—wise people do not cling to them for ever.'

Instead of simply despising this Indian view of life, might we not pause for a moment and consider whether their philosophy of life is entirely wrong, and ours entirely right; whether this earth was really meant for work only (for with us pleasure also has been changed into work), for constant hurry and flurry; or whether we, sturdy Northern Aryas, might not have been satisfied with a little less of work, and a little less of so-called pleasure, but with a little more of thought, and a little more of rest. For, short as our life is, we are not mere Mayflies that are born in the morning to die at night. We have a past to look back to and a future to look forward to, and it may be that some of the riddles of the future find their solution in the wisdom of the past.

Then why should we always fix our eyes on the present only? Why should we always be racing, whether for wealth or for power or for fame? Why should we never rest and be thankful?

I do not deny that the manly vigour, the silent endurance, the public spirit, and the private virtues too of the citizens of European states represent one side, it may be a very important side, of the destiny which man has to fulfil on earth.

But there is surely another side of our nature, and possibly another destiny open to man in his journey across this life, which should not be entirely ignored. If we turn our eyes to the East, and particularly to India, where life is, or at all events was, no very severe struggle, where the climate was mind, the soil fertile, where vegetable food in small quantities sufficed to keep the body in health and strength, where the simplest hut or cave in a forest was all the shelter required, and where social life never assumed the gigantic, aye, monstrous proportions of a London or Paris, but fulfilled itself within the narrow boundaries of village communities,—was it not, I say, natural there, or, if you like, was it not *intended* there, that another side of human nature should be developed—not the active, the combative and acquisitive, but the passive, the meditative and reflective? Can we wonder that the Aryas who stepped as strangers into some of the happy fields and valleys along the Indus or the Ganges should have looked upon life as a perpetual Sunday or holyday, or a kind of long vacation, delightful so long as it lasts, but which must come to an end sooner or later? Why should they have accumulated wealth? Why should they have built palaces? Why should they have toiled day and night? After having provided from day to day for the small necessities of the body, they thought they had the right, it may be the duty, to look round upon this strange exile, to look inward upon themselves, upward to something not themselves, and to see whether they could not understand a little of the true purport of that mystery which we call life on earth.

Of course *we* should call such notions of life dreamy, unreal, unpractical, but may not *they* look upon our notions of life as short-sighted, fussy, and, in the end, most unpractical, because involving a sacrifice of life for the sake of life?

No doubt these are both extreme views, and they have hardly ever been held or realised in that extreme form by any nation, whether in the East or in the West. We are not always plodding—we sometimes allow ourselves an hour of rest and peace and thought—nor were the ancient people of India always dreaming and meditating on *ta megista*, on the great problems of life, but, when called upon, we know that they too could fight like heroes, and that, without machinery, they could by patient toil raise even the meanest handiwork into a work of art, a real joy to the maker and to the buyer.

All then that I wish to put clearly before you is this, that the Aryan man, who had to fulfil his mission in India, might naturally be deficient in many of the practical and fighting virtues, which wear developed in the Northern Aryas by the very struggle without which they could not have survived, but that his life on earth had not therefore been entirely wasted. His very view of life, though we cannot adopt it in this Northern climate, may yet act as a lesson and a warning to us, not, for the sake of life, to sacrifice the highest objects of life.

The greatest conqueror of antiquity stood in silent wonderment before the Indian Gymnosophists, regretting that he could not communicate with them in their own language, and that their wisdom could not reach him except through the containing channels of sundry interpreters.

That need not be so at present. Sanskrit is no longer a difficult language, and I can assure every young Indian Civil Servant that if he will but go to the fountain-head of Indian wisdom, he will find there, among much that is strange and useless, some lessons of life which are worth learning, and which we in our haste are too apt to forget or to despise.

Let me read you a few sayings only, which you may still hear repeated in India, when, after the heat of the day, the old and the young assemble together under the shadow of their village tree—sayings which to them seem truth, to us, I fear, mere truism!

'As all have to sleep together laid low in the earth, why do foolish people with to injure one another?'

'A man seeking for eternal happiness (*moksha*) might obtain it by a hundredth part of the sufferings which a foolish man endures in the pursuit of riches.'

'Poor men eat more excellent bread than the rich: for hunger gives it sweetness.'

'Our body is like the foam of the sea, our life like a bird, our company with those whom we love does not last for ever; why then sleepest thou, my son?'

'As two logs of wood meet upon the ocean and then separate again, thus do living creatures meet.'

'Family, wife, children, our very body and our wealth, they all pass away. They do not belong to us. What then is ours?—Our good and our evil deeds.'

'When thou goest away from here, no one will follow thee. Only thy good and thy evil deeds they will follow thee wherever thou goest.'

'According to the Veda the soul (life) is eternal, but the body of all creatures is perishable. When the body is destroyed, the soul departs elsewhere, fettered by the bonds of our works.'

'As a man puts on new garments in this world, throwing aside those which he formerly wore, even so the Self of man puts on new bodies which are in accordance with his acts.'

'No weapons will hurt the Self of man, no fire will burn it, no water moisten it, no wind will dry it up.'

'It is not to be hurt, not to be burnt, not to be moistened, not to be dried up. It is imperishable, unchanging, immovable, without beginning.'

'It is said to be immaterial, passing all understanding, and unchangeable. If you know the Self of man to be all this, grieve not.'

'There is nothing higher than the attainment of the knowledge of the Self.'

'All living creatures are the dwelling of the Self who lies enveloped in matter, who is immortal, and spotless. Those who worship the Self, the immovable, living in a movable dwelling, become immortal.'

'Despising everything else, a wise man should strive after the knowledge of the Self.'

We shall have to return to this subject again, for this knowledge of the Self is really the Vedanta, that is, the end, the highest goal of the Veda. The highest wisdom of Greece was 'to know ourselves;' the highest wisdom of India is 'to know our Self.'

If I were asked to indicate by one word the distinguishing feature of the Indian character, as I have here tried to sketch it, I should say it was *transcendent*, using that word, not in its strict technical sense, as fixed by Kant, but in its more general acceptation, as denoting a mind bent on transcending the limits of empirical knowledge. There are minds perfectly satisfied with empirical knowledge, a knowledge of facts, well ascertained, well classified, and well labelled. Such knowledge may assume very vast proportions, and, if knowledge is power, it may impart great power, real intellectual power to the man who can wield and utilise it. Our own age is proud of that kind of knowledge, and to be content with it, and never to attempt to look beyond it, is, I believe, one of the happiest states of mind to be in.

But, for all that, there is a Beyond, and he who has once caught a glance of it, is like a man who has gazed at the sun—wherever he looks, everywhere he sees the image of the sun. Speak to him of finite things, and he will tell you that the Finite is impossible and meaningless without the Infinite. Speak to him of death, and he will call it birth; speak to him of time, and he will call it the mere shadow of eternity. To us the senses seem to be the organs, the tools, the most powerful engines of knowledge; to him they are, if not actually deceivers, at all events heavy fetters, checking the flight of the spirit. To us this earth, this life, all that we see, and hear, and touch is certain. Here, we feel, is our home, here lie our duties, here our pleasures. To him this earth is a thing that once was not, and that again will cease to be; this life is a short dream from which we shall soon awake. Of nothing he professes greater ignorance than of what to others seems to be most certain, namely what we see, and hear, and touch; and as to our home, wherever that may be, he knows that certainly it is not here.

Do not suppose that such men are mere dreamers. Far from it! And if we can only bring ourselves to be quite honest to ourselves, we shall have to confess that at times we all have been visited by these transcendental aspirations, and have been able to understand what Wordsworth meant when he spoke of those

'Obstinate questionings
Of sense and outward things,

Fallings from us, vanishings;
Blank misgivings of a creature
Moving about in worlds not realised.'

The transcendent temperament acquired no doubt a more complete supremacy in the Indian character than anywhere else: but no nation, and no individual, is entirely without that 'yearning beyond;' indeed we all know it under a more familiar name—namely, *Religion.*

It is necessary, however, to distinguish between religion and a religion, quite as much as in another branch of philosophy we have to distinguish between language and *a* language or many languages. A man may accept *a* religion, he may be converted to the Christian religion, and he may change his own particular religion from time to time, just as he may speak different languages. But in order to have *a* religion, a man must have religion. He must once *at least* in his life have looked beyond the horizon of this world, and carried away in his mind an impression of the Infinite, which will never leave him again. A being satisfied with the world of sense, unconscious of its finite nature, undisturbed by the limited or negative character of all perceptions of the senses, would be incapable of any religious concepts. Only when the finite character of all human knowledge has been perceived, is it possible for the human mind to conceive that which is beyond the Finite, call it what you like, the Beyond, the Unseen, the Infinite, the Supernatural, or the Divine. That step must have been taken before religion of any kind becomes possible. What kind of religion it will be, depends on the character of the race which elaborates it, its surroundings in nature, and its experience in history.

Now we may seem to know a great many religions—I speak here, of course, of ancient religions only, of what are sometimes called national or autochthonous religions—not of those founded in later times by individual prophets or reformers.

Yet, among those ancient religions we seldom know, what after all is the most important point, their origin and their gradual growth. The Jewish religion is represented to us as perfect and complete from the very first, and it is with great difficulty that we can discover its real beginnings and its historical growth. And take the Greek and the Roman religions, take the religions of the Teutonic, Slavonic or Celtic tribes, and you will find that their period of growth has always passed, long before we know them, and that from the time we know them, all their changes are purely *metamorphic*—changes in form of substances ready at hand.

Now let us look to the ancient inhabitants of India. With them, first of all, religion was not only *one* interest by the side of many. It was the all-absorbing interest; it embraced not only worship and prayer, but what we call philosophy, morality, law, and government,—all was pervaded by religion. Their whole life was to them a religion—everything else was, as it were, a mere concession made to the ephemeral requirements of this life.

What then can we learn from the ancient religious literature of India—or from the Veda?

It requires no very profound knowledge of Greek religion and Greek language to discover in the Greek deities the original outlines of certain physical phenomena. Every schoolboy knows that in *Zeus* there is something of the sky, in *Poseidon* of the sea, in *Hades* of the lower world, in *Apollo* of the sun, in *Artemis* of the moon, in *Hephœstos* of the fire. But for all that, there is, from a Greek point of view, a very considerable difference between *Zeus* and the sky, between *Poseidon* and the sea, between *Apollo* and the sun, between *Artemis* and the moon.

Now what do we find in the Veda? No doubt here and there a few philosophical hymns which have been quoted so often that people have begun to imagine that the Vedas is a kind of collection of Orphic hymns. We also find some purely mythological hymns, in which the Devas or gods have assumed nearly as much dramatic personality as in the Homeric hymns.

But the great majority of Vedic hymns consists in simple invocations of the fire, the water, the sky, the sun, and the storms, often under the same names which afterwards became the proper names of Hindu deities, but as yet nearly free from all that can be called irrational or mythological. There is nothing irrational, nothing I mean we cannot enter into or sympathise with, in people imploring the storms to cease, or the sky to rain, or the sun to shine. I say there is nothing irrational in it, though perhaps it might be more accurate to say that there is nothing in it that would surprise anybody who is acquainted with the growth of human reason, or, at all events, of childish reason. It does not matter how we call the tendency of the childish mind to confound the manifestation with that which manifests itself, effect with cause, act with agent. Call it Animism, Personification, Metaphor, or Poetry, we all know what is meant by it, in the most general sense of all these names; we all know that it exists, and the youngest child who beats the chair against which he has fallen; or who scolds his dog, or who sings, 'Rain, rain, go to Spain,' can teach us that, however irrational all this may seem to us, it is perfectly rational, natural, aye inevitable in the first periods, or the childish age of the human mind.

Now it is exactly this period in the growth of ancient religion, which was always presupposed, or postulated, but was absent everywhere else, that is clearly put before us in the hymns of the *Rigveda*. It is this ancient chapter in the history of the human mind which has been preserved to us in Indian literature, while we look for it in vain in Greece or Rome or elsewhere.

It has been a favourite idea of those who call themselves 'students of man,' or anthropologists, that in order to know the earliest or so-called prehistoric phases in the growth of man, we should study the life of savage nations, as we may watch it still in some parts of Asia, Africa, Polynesia, and America.

There is much truth in this, and nothing can be more useful than the observations which we find collected in the works of such students as Waitz, Tylor, Lubbock, and many others. But let us be honest, and confess, first of all, that the materials on which we have here to depend are often extremely untrustworthy.

Nor is this all. What do we know of savage tribes beyond the latest chapter of their history? Do we ever get an insight into their antecedents? Can we understand, what after all is everywhere the most important and the most instructive lesson to learn, how they have come to be what they are? There is indeed their language, and in it we see traces of growth that point to distant ages, quite as much as the Greek of Homer, or the Sanskrit of the Vedas. Their language proves indeed that these so-called heathens, with their complicated systems of mythology, their artificial customs, their unintelligible whims and savageries, are not the creatures of today or yesterday. Unless we admit a special creation for these savages, they must be as old as the Hindus, the Greeks and Romans, as old as we ourselves. We may assume, of course, if we like, that their life has been stationary, and that they are today what the Hindus were no longer 3,000 years ago. But that is a mere guess, and is contradicted by the facts of their language. They may have passed through ever so many vicissitudes, and what we consider as primitive may be, for all we know, a relapse into savagery, or a corruption of something that was more rational and intelligible in former stages. Think only of the rules that determine marriage among the lowest of savage tribes. Their complication passes all understanding, all seems a chaos of prejudice, superstition, pride, vanity and stupidity. And yet we catch a glimpse here and there that there was some reason in most of that unreason; we see how sense dwindled away into nonsense, custom into ceremony, ceremony into farce. Why then should this surface of savage life represent to us the lowest stratum of human life, the very beginnings of civilization, simply because we cannot dig beyond that surface?

Now, I do not wish to be misunderstood. I do not claim for the ancient Indian literature any more than I should willingly concede to the fables and traditions and songs of savage nations, such as we can study at present in what we call a state of nature. Both are important documents to the student of the Science of Man. I simply say that in the Veda we have a nearer approach to a beginning, and an intelligible beginning, than in the wild invocations of Hottentots or Bushmen. But when I speak of a beginning. I do not mean an absolute beginning, a beginning of all things. Again and again the question has been asked whether we could bring ourselves to believe that man, as soon as he could stand on his legs, instead of crawling on all fours, as he is supposed to have done, burst forth into singing Vedic hymns? But who has ever maintained this? Surely whoever has eyes to see can see in every Vedic hymn, aye, in every Vedic word, as many rings within rings as in the oldest tree that was ever hewn down in the forest.

I shall say even more, and I have said it before, namely, that supposing that the Vedic hymns were composed between 1500 and 1000 BC, we can hardly understand how, at so early a date, the Indians had developed ideas which to us sound decidedly modern. I should give anything if I could escape from the conclusion that the collection of the Vedic Hymns, a collection in ten books, existed at least 1000 BC, that is about 500 years before the rise of Buddhism. I do not mean to say that something may not be discovered hereafter to enable us to refer that collection to a later date. All I say is that, so far as we know *at present*, so far as all honest Sanskrit scholars know *at present*, we cannot well bring our pre-Buddhistic literature into narrower limits than 500 years.

What then is to be done? We must simply keep our pre-conceived notions of what people call primitive humanity in abeyance for a time, and if we find that people three thousand years ago were familiar with ideas that seem novel and nineteenth-century-like to us, well, we must somewhat modify our conceptions of the primitive savage, and remember that things hid from the wise and prudent have sometimes been revealed to babes.

I maintain then that for a study of man, or, if you like, for a study of Aryan humanity, there is nothing in the world equal in importance with the Veda. I maintain that to everybody who cares for himself, for his ancestors, for his history, or for his intellectual development, a study of Vedic literature is indispensable; and that, as an element of liberal education, it is far more important and far more improving than the reigns of Babylonian and Persian kings, aye even than the dates and deeds of many of the kings of Judah and Israel.

It is curious to observe the reluctance with which these facts are accepted, particularly by those to whom they ought to be most welcome. I mean the students of anthropology. Instead of devoting all their energy of the study of these documents, which have come upon us like a miracle, they seem only bent on inventing excuses why they need not be studied. Let it not be supposed that, because there are several translations of the *Rigveda* in English, French, and German, therefore all that the Veda can teach us has been learned. Far from it. Every one of these translations has been put forward as tentative only. I myself, though during the last thirty years I have given translations of a number of the more important hymns, have only ventured to publish a specimen of what I think a translation of the Veda ought to be; and that translation, that *traduction raisonnee* as I ventured to call it, of twelve hymns only, fills a whole volume. We are still on the mere surface of Vedic literature, and yet our critics are ready with ever so many arguments why the Veda can teach us nothing as to a primitive state of man. If they mean by primitive that which came absolutely first, then they ask for something which they will never get, not even if they discovered the private correspondence of Adam and Eve, or of the first *Homo* and *Femina sapiens*. We mean by primitive the earliest state of man of which, from the nature of the case, we can hope to gain any knowledge; and here, next to the archives hidden away in the secret drawers of language in the treasury of words common to all the Aryan tribes, and in the radical elements of which each word is compounded, there is no literary relic more full of lessons to the true anthropologist, to the true student of mankind, than the *Rigveda*.

Notes

Pages

52. **Dante** (1265-1321): One of the greatest of European poets; his *Divina Comedia* was the first literary work in Italian.

55. **The Renaissance Period of Indian literature:** Max Müller held that from the first century BC there was a lull in literary activity in Sanskrit which remained unbroken till the end of the third century AD when there was this 'Renaissance'. This theory no longer finds acceptance, and the growth of Sanskrit literature is seen to have been a more continuous process than was believed by Max Müller. Macdonell, *Sanskrit Literature,* p. 323; Keith, *A History of Sanskrit Literature,* p. 39. But the differences between Vedic literature and the later classical Sanskrit literature noted by Max Müller still hold good.

55. **Dayananda** (Dayananda Sarasvati, 1827-83): Founder of the Arya Samaj. He regarded the Vedas, at least the *mantra* portion, as divine revelations, and as a reformer, he was opposed to post-Vedic abuses.

57. **Kanishka:** The most celebrated of the Yueh-chi (Kushan) rulers of India. Early second century AD is the date now generally accepted for him. He was a patron of Sanskrit learning as well as of Buddhism.

57. **Sutras:** Manuals composed in an aphoristic style.
Itihasas and Akhyanas: Tales and narratives purporting to historical.
Puranas: A series of eighteen long works dealing with the creation of the world, the dynasties of kings, etc.

58. **Kalidasa:** Sanskrit poet and dramatist; beginning of the fifth century AD.
Hitopadesa: 'Useful instruction'—name of a collecton of fables, apologues and moral stories meant for the education of children.
Bhartrihari: Sanskrit poet and grammarian, died about AD 650. Policy, Love, and Renunciation formed the subjects each of a hundred verses by him.
A. Humboldt (1769-1859): Celebrated German naturalist and scholar, and one of the creators of botanical geography. His *Cosmos* is an attempt to give a physical description of the world.

59. **Justinian:** Emperor of Constantinople, AD 527-65. Codified Roman Law.
Varahamihira: Celebrated Hindu astronomer, author of the *Brihat-Samhita.*

61. **Burnouf:** (Eugene, 1801-52): Founder of the Societe Asiatique in Paris; edited and translated the *Bhagavata* and translated the *Saddharma Pundarika,* the Lotus of the Good Law, a Buddhist classic. The first to study the Zend language and the old Persian cuneiform inscriptions. Max Müller was one of his pupils.

65. **Gymnosophists:** Ancient Hindu ascetics whom Alexander met.

70. **Waitz:** German anthropologist who published an important work in 1859.
Tylor (Sir E.B.): } Famous English Anthropologists of the
Lubbock (John, Lord Avebury): } 19th century.

71. **something . . . . to a later date :** On the other hand recent research points to an earlier date. Winternitz, *History of Indian Literature* (vol. I, p. 310) assigns the Vedic hymns to 2500 BC.

Lecture IV

Was Vedic Culture Exclusive?

It may be quite true that controversy often does more harm than good, that it encourages the worst of all talents, that of plausibility, not to say dishonesty, and generally leaves the world at large worse confounded than it was before. It has been said that no clever lawyer would shrink from taking a brief to prove that the earth forms the centre of the world, and, with all respect for English Juries, it is not impossible that even in our days he might gain a verdict against Galileo. I do not deny that there is a power and vitality in truth which in the end overcomes and survives all opposition, as shown by the very doctrine of Galileo which at present is held by hundreds and thousands who would find it extremely difficult to advance one single argument in its support. I am ready to admit also that those who have done the best work, and have contributed most largely toward the advancement of knowledge and the progress of truth, have seldom wasted their time in controversy, but have marched on straight, little concerned either about applause on the right or abuse on the left. All this is true, perfectly true, and yet I feel that I cannot escape from devoting the whole of a lecture to the answering of certain objections which have been raised against the views which I have put forward with regard to the character and the historical importance of Vedic literature. We must not forget that the whole subject is new, the number of competent judges small, and mistakes not only possible, but almost inevitable. Besides, there are mistakes and mistakes, and the errors of able men are often instructive, nay one might say sometimes almost indispensable for the discovery of truth. There are criticisms which may be safely ignored, criticisms for the sake of criticism, if not inspired by meaner motives. But there are doubts and difficulties which suggest themselves naturally, objections which have a right to be heard, and the very removal of which forms the best approach to the stronghold of truth. Nowhere has this principle been so fully recognised and been acted on as in Indian literature. Whatever subject is started, the rule is that the argument should begin with the cons, so-called Purvapaksha, with all that can be said against a certain opinion. Every possible objection is welcome, if only it is not altogether frivolous and absurd, and then only follow the pros, the Uttarapaksha, with all that can be said against these objections and in support of the original opinion. Only when this process has been fully gone through is it allowed to represent an opinion as *siddhanta*, or established.

Therefore, before opening the pages of the Veda, and giving you a description of the poetry, the religion, and philosophy of ancient inhabitants of India, I thought it right and necessary to establish, first of all, certain points without which it would be impossible to form a right appreciation of the historical value of the Vedic hymns, and of their importance even to us who live at so great a distance from those early poets.

The *first* point was purely preliminary, namely that the Hindus in ancient, and in modern times also, are a nation deserving of our interest and sympathy, worthy also of our confidence, and by no means guilty of the charge so recklessly brought against them—the charge of an habitual disregard of truth.

Secondly, that the ancient literature of India is not to be considered simply as a curiosity and to be handed over to the good pleasure of Oriental scholars, but that, both by its language, the Sanskrit, and by its most ancient literary documents, the Vedas, it can teach us lessons which nothing else can teach, as to the origin of our own language, the first formation of our own concepts, and the true natural germs of all that is comprehended under the name of civilization, at least the civilization of the Aryan race, that race to which we and all the greatest nations of the world—the Hindus, the Persians, the Greeks and Romans, the Slavs, the Celts, and last, not least, the Teutons, belong. A man may be a good and useful ploughman without being a geologist, without knowing the stratum on which he takes his stand, or the strata beneath, which give support to the soil whereon he lives and works, and from whence he draws his nourishment. And a man may be a good and useful citizen, without being an historian, without knowing how the world in which he lives came about, and how many phases mankind had to pass through in language, religion, and philosophy, before it could supply him with that intellectual soil on which he himself lives and works, and from which he draws his best nourishments.

But there must always be an aristocracy of those who know, and who can trace back the best which we possess, not merely to a Norman Count, or a Scandinavian Viking, or a Saxon Earl, but to far older ancestors and benefactors, who thousands of years ago were toiling for us in the sweat of their face, and without whom we should never be what we are,— the ancestors of the whole Aryan race, the first framers of our words, the first poets of our thoughts, the first givers of our laws, the first prophets of our gods, and of Him who is God above all gods.

That aristocracy of those who know,—*di color che sanno,*—or try to know, is open to all who are willing to enter, to all who have a feeling for the past, an interest in the pedigree of our thoughts, and a reverence for the ancestry of our intellect, who are in fact historians in the true sense of the word, i.e. inquirers into that which is past, but not lost.

Thirdly, having explained to you why the ancient literature of India, the really ancient literature of that country, I mean that of the Vedic period, deserves the careful attention, not of Oriental scholars only, but of every educated man and woman who wishes to know how we, even we here in England and in this nineteenth century of ours, came to be what we are, I tried to explain to you the difference, the natural and inevitable difference, between the development of the human character in such different climates as those of India and Europe. And while admitting that the Hindus were deficient in many of those manly virtues and practical achievements which we value most, I wished to point out that there was another sphere of intellectual activity in which the Hindus excelled—the meditative and transcendent—and that here we might learn from them some lessons of life which we ourselves are but too apt to ignore or to despise.

Fourthly, fearing that I might have raised too high expectations of the ancient wisdom, the religion and philosophy of the Vedic Indians, I felt it my duty to state that, though primitive in one sense, we must not expect the Vedic religion to be primitive in the anthropological sense of the word, as containing the utterances of beings who had just broken their shells, and were wonderingly looking out for the first time upon this strange world. The Veda may be called primitive, because there is no other literary document more primitive than it: but the language, the mythology, the religion and philosophy that meet us in the Veda open vistas of the past which no one would venture measure in years. Nay, they contain, by the side of simple, natural, childish thoughts, many ideas which to us sound modern, or secondary and tertiary, as I called them, but which nevertheless are older than any other literary document, and give us trustworthy information of a period in the history of human thought of which we knew absolutely nothing before the discovery of the Vedas.

But even thus our path is not yet clear. Other objections have been raised against the Veda as an historical document. Some of them are important; and I have at times shared them myself. Others are at least instructive, and will give us an opportunity of testing the foundation on which we stand.

The first objection then against our treating the Veda as an historical document is that it is not truly national in its character, and dose not represent the thoughts of the whole of the population of India, but only of a small minority, namely of the Brahmans, and not even of the whole class of Brahmans, but only of a small minority of them, namely of the professional priests.

Objections should not be based on demands which, from the nature of the case, are unreasonable. Have those who maintain that the Vedic hymns do not represent the whole of India, that is the whole of its ancient population, in the same manner as they say that the *Bible* represents the Jews or Homer the Greeks, considered what they are asking for? So far from denying that the Vedic hymns represent only a small and, it may be, a priestly minority of the ancient population of India, the true historian would probably feel inclined to urge the same cautions against the *Old Testament* and the Homeric poems also.

No doubt, after the books which compose the *Old Testament* had been collected as a Sacred Canon, they were known to the majority of the Jews. But when we speak of the primitive state of the Jews, of their moral, intellectual, and religious status while in Mesopotamia or Canaan or Egypt, we should find that the different books of the *Old Testament* teach us as little of the whole Jewish race, with all its local characteristics and social distinctions, as the Homeric poems do of all the Greek tribes, or the Vedic hymns of all the inhabitants of India. Surely, even when we speak of the history of the Greeks or the Romans, we know that we shall not find there a complete picture of the social, intellectual, and religious life of a whole nation. We know very little of the intellectual life of a whole nation, even during the Middle Ages, aye even at the present day. We may know something of the generals, of the commanders-in-chief, but of the privates, of the millions, we know next to nothing. And what we do know of kings or generals or ministers is mostly no more than what was thought of them by a few Greek poets or Jewish prophets, men who were one in a million among their contemporaries.

But it might be said that though the writers were few, the readers were many. Is that so? I believe you would be surprised to hear how small the number of readers is even in modern times, while in ancient times reading was restricted to the very smallest class of privileged persons. There may have been listeners at public and private festivals, at sacrifices, and later on in theatres, but readers, in our sense of the word, are a very modern invention.

There never has been so much reading, reading spread over so large an area, as in our times. But if you asked publishers as to the number of copies sold of books which are supposed to have been read by everybody, say Macaulay's *History of England, The Life of the Prince Consort*, or Darwin's *Origin of Species*, you would find that out of a population of thirty-two millions not one million has possessed itself of a copy of these works. The book which of late has probably had the largest sale is the revised version of the *New Testament*; and yet the whole number of copies sold among the eighty millions of English-speaking people is probably not more than four millions. Of ordinary books which are called books of the season, and which are supposed to have had a great success, an edition of three or four thousand copies is not considered unsatisfactory by either publishers or authors in England. But if you look to other countries, such, for instance, as Russia, it would be very difficult indeed to name books that could be considered as representative of the whole nation, or as even known by more than a very small minority.

And if we turn our thoughts back to the ancient nations of Greece and Italy, or of Persia and Babylonia, what book is there, with the exception perhaps of the Homeric poems, of which we could say that it had been read or even heard of by more than a few thousand people? We think of Greeks and Romans as literary people, and so no doubt they were, but in a very different sense from what we mean by this. What we call Greeks and Romans are chiefly the citizens of Athens and Rome, and here again those who could produce or who could read such works as the *Dialogues of Plato* or the *Epistles of Horace* constituted a very small intellectual aristocracy indeed. What we call history—the memory of past—has always been the work of minorities. Millions and millions pass away unheeded, and the few only to whom has been given the gift of fusing speech and thought into forms of beauty remain as witnesses of the past.

If then we speak of times so distant as those represented by the *Rigveda,* and of a country so disintegrated, or rather as yet so little integrated as India was three thousand years ago, surely it requires but little reflection to know that what we see in the Vedic poems are but a few snow-clad peaks, representing to us, from a far distance, the whole mountain-range of a nation, completely lost beyond the horizon of history. When we speak of the Vedic hymns as representing the religion, the thoughts and customs of India three thousand years ago, we cannot mean by India more than some unknown quantity of which the poets of the Veda are the only spokesmen left. When we now speak of India, we think of 250 millions, a sixth part of the whole human race, peopling the vast peninsula from the Himalayan mountains between the arms of the Indus and the Ganges, down to Cape Comorin and Ceylon, an extent of country nearly as large as Europe. In the Veda the stage on which the life of the ancient kings and poets is acted, is the valley of the Indus and the Punjab, as it is now called, the Sapta Sindhavah, the Seven Rivers of the Vedic poets. The land watered by the Ganges is hardly known, and the whole of the Dekkan seems not yet to have been discovered.

Then again, when these Vedic hymns are called the lucubrations of a few priests, not the outpourings of the genius of a whole nation, what does that mean? We may no doubt call these ancient Vedic poets priests, if we like, and no one would deny that their poetry is pervaded not only by religious, mythological, and philosophical, but likewise by sacrificial and ceremonial conceits. Still a priest, if we trace him back far enough, is only a *presbyteros* or an elder, and, as such, those Vedic poets had a perfect right to speak in the name of a whole class or of the village community to which they belonged. Call Vasishtha a priest by all means, only do not let us imagine that he was therefore something like Cardinal Manning.

After we have made every possible concession to arguments, most of which are purely hypothetical, there remains this great fact that here, in the *Rigveda*, we have poems, composed in perfect language, in elaborate metre, telling us about gods and men, about sacrifices and battles, about the varying aspects of nature and the changing conditions of society, about duty and pleasure, philosophy and morality—articulate voices reaching us from a distance from which we never heard before the faintest whisper; and instead of thrilling with delight at this almost miraculous discovery, some critics stand aloof and can do nothing but find fault, because these songs do not represent to us primitive men exactly as they think they ought to have been; not like Papuas or Bushmen, with arboraceous habits and half-bestial clicks, not as worshipping stocks or stones, or believing in fetishes, as according to Comte's inner consciousness they ought to have done, but rather, I must confess, as beings whom we can understand, with whom to a certain extent we can sympathise, and to whom, in the historical progress of the human intellect, we may assign a place, not very far behind the ancient Jews and Greeks.

Once more then, if we mean by primitive, people who inhabited this earth as soon as the vanishing of the glacial period made this earth inhabitable, the Vedic poets were certainly not primitive. If we mean by primitive, people who were without a knowledge of fire, who used unpolished flints, and ate raw flesh, the Vedic poets were not primitive. If we mean by primitive, people who did not cultivate the soil, had no fixed abodes, no kings, no sacrifices, no laws, again, I say, the Vedic poets were not primitive. But if we mean by primitive the people who have been the first of the Aryan race to leave behind literary relics of their existence on earth, then I say the Vedic poets are primitive, the Vedic language is primitive, the Vedic religion is primitive, and, taken as a whole, more primitive than anything else that we are ever likely to recover in the whole history of our race.

When all these objections had failed, a last trump was played. The ancient Vedic poetry was said to be, if not of foreign origin, at least very much infected by foreign, and more particularly by Semitic influences. It had always been urged by Sanskrit scholars as one of the chief attractions of Vedic literature that it not only allowed us an insight into a very early phase of religious thought, but that the Vedic religion was the only one the development of which took place without any extraneous influences, and could be watched through a longer series of centuries than any other religion. Now with regard to the first point, we know how perplexing it is in the religion of ancient Rome to distinguish between Italian and Greek ingredients, to say nothing of Etruscan and Phoenician influences. We know the difficulty of finding out in the religion of the Greeks what is purely home-grown, and what is taken over from Egypt, Phœnicia, it may be, from Scythia; or at all events, slightly coloured by those foreign rays of thought. Even in the religion of the Hebrews, Babylonian, Phœnician, and at a later time Persian influences have been discovered, and the more we advance towards modern times, the more extensive becomes the mixture of thought, and the more difficult the task of assigning to each nation the share which it contributed to the common intellectual currency of the world. In India alone, and more particularly in Vedic India, we see a plant entirely grown on native soil, and entirely nurtured by native air. For this reason, because the religion of the Veda was so completely guarded from all strange infections, it is full of lessons which the student of religion could learn nowhere else.

Now what have the critics of the Veda to say against this? They say that the Vedic poems show clear traces of Babylonian influences.

I must enter into some details, because, small as they seem, you can see that they involve very wide consequences.

There is one verse in the *Rigveda*, which has been translated as follows: 'O Indra, bring to us a brilliant jewel, a cow, a horse, an ornament, together with a golden Mana.'

Now what is a golden Mana? The word does not occur again by itself, either in the Veda or anywhere else, and it has been identified by Vedic scholars with the Latin *mina*, the Greek *mna*, the Phœnician *manah*, the well-known weight which we actually possess now among the treasures brought from Babylon and Nineveh to the British Museum.

If this were so, it would be irrefragable evidence of at all events a commercial intercourse between Babylon and India at a very early time, though it would in no way prove a real influence of Semitic on Indian thought. But is it so? Although the passage is difficult, because *mana* does not occur again in the *Rigveda*, I should think we might take *mana hiranyaya* for a dual, and translate, 'Give us also two golden armlets.' To suppose that the Vedic poets should have borrowed this one word and this one measure from the Babylonians, would be against all the rules of historical criticism. The word *mana* never occurs again in the whole of Sanskrit literature, no other Babylonian weight occurs again in the whole of Sanskrit literature, and it is not likely that a poet who asks for a cow and a horse, would ask in the same breath for a foreign weight of gold, that is, for about sixty sovereigns.

But this is not the only loan that India has been supposed to have negotiated in Babylon. The twenty-seven Nakshatras, or the twenty-seven constellations, which were chosen in India as a kind of lunar Zodiac, were supposed to have come from Babylon. Now the Babylonian Zodiac was solar, and, in spite of repeated researches no trace of a lunar Zodiac has been found, where so many things have been found, in the cuneiform inscriptions. But supposing even that a lunar Zodiac had been discovered in Babylon, no one acquainted with Vedic literature and with the ancient Vedic ceremonial would easily allow himself to be persuaded that the Hindus had borrowed that simple division of the sky from the Babylonians. It is well known that most of the Vedic sacrifices depend on the moon, far more than on the sun. As the Psalmist says, 'He appointed the moon for seasons; the sun knoweth his going down,' we read in the *Rigveda* in a verse addressed to sun and moon, 'They walk by their own power, one after the other (or from east to west), as playing children they go round the sacrifice. The one looks upon all the worlds, the other is born again and again, determining the seasons.'

'He becomes new and new, when he is born; as the herald of the days, he goes before the dawns. By his approach he determines their share for the gods; the moon increases a long life.'

The moon, then, determines the seasons, the ritus, the moon fixes the share, that is, the sacrificial oblation for all the gods. The seasons and the sacrifices were in fact so intimately connected together in the thoughts of the ancient Hindus, that one of the commonest names for priests was *ritvig*, literally, the season-sacrificer.

Besides the rites which have to be performed every day, such as the five Mahayajnas, and the Agnihotra in the morning and the evening, the important sacrifices in Vedic times were the Full and New-moon sacrifices; the Season-sacrifices, each season consisting of four months; and the Half-yearly sacrifices, at the two solstices. There are other sacrifices to be performed in autumn and summer, others in winter and spring, whenever rice and barley are ripening.

The regulation of the seasons, as one of the fundamental conditions of an incipient society, seems in fact to have been so intimately connected with the worship of the gods, as the guardians of the seasons and the protectors of law and order, that it is sometimes difficult to say whether in their stated sacrifices the maintenance of the calendar or the maintenance of the worship of gods was more prominent in the minds of the old Vedic priests.

The twenty-seven Nakshatras then were clearly suggested by the moon's passage. Nothing was more natural for the sake of counting days, months, or seasons than to observe the twenty-seven places which the moon occupied in her passage from any point of the sky back to the same point. It was far easier than to determine the sun's position either from day to day, or from month to month; for the stars, being hardly visible at the actual rising and setting of the sun, the idea of the sun's conjunction with certain stars could not suggest itself to a listless observer. The moon, on the contrary, progressing from night to night, and coming successively in contact with certain stars, was like the finger of a clock, moving round a circle, and coming in contact with one figure after another on the dial-plate of the sky. Nor would the portion of about one-third of a lunation in addition to the twenty-seven stars from new moon to new moon, create much confusion in the minds of the rough-and-ready reckoners of those early times. All they were concerned with were the twenty-seven celestial stations which, after being once traced out by the moon, were fixed, like so many mile-stones, for determining the course of all the celestial travellers that could be of any interest for signs and for seasons, and for days and for years. A circle divided into twenty-seven sections, or any twenty-seven poles planted in a circle at equal distances round a house, would answer the purpose of a primitive Vedic observatory. All that was wanted to be known was between which pair of poles the moon, or afterwards the sun also, was visible at their rising or setting, the observer occupying the same central position on every day.

Our notions of astronomy cannot in fact be too crude and too imperfect if we wish to understand the first beginnings in the reckoning of days and seasons and years. We cannot expect in those days more than what any shepherd would know at present of the sun and moon, the stars and seasons. Nor can we expect any observations of heavenly phenomena unless they had some bearing on the practical wants of primitive society.

If then we can watch in India the natural, nay inevitable, growth of the division of the heaven into twenty-seven equal divisions, each division marked by stars, which may have been observed and named long before they were used for this new purpose—if, on the other hand, we could hardly understand the growth and development of the Indian ceremonial except as determined by a knowledge of the lunar asterisms, the lunar months, and the lunar seasons, surely it would be a senseless hypothesis to imagine that the Vedic shepherds or priests went to Babylonia in search of a knowledge which every shepherd might have acquired on the banks of the Indus, and that, after their return from that country only, where a language was spoken which no Hindu could understand, they set to work to compose their sacred hymns, and arrange their simple ceremonial. We must never forget that what is natural in one place is natural in other places also, and we may sum up without fear of serious contradiction, that no case has been made out in favour of a foreign origin of the elementary astronomical notions of the Hindus as found or presupposed in the Vedic hymns.

The Arabs, as is well known, have twenty-eight lunar stations, the *Manzil*, and I can see no reason why Mohammed and his Bedouins in the desert should not have made the same observation as the Vedic poets in India, though I must admit at the same time that Colebrooke has brought forward very cogent arguments to prove that, in their scientific employment at least, the Arabic *Manzil* were really borrowed from an Indian source.

The Chinese, too, have their famous lunar stations, the *Sieu*, originally twenty-four in number, and afterwards raised to twenty-eight. But here again there is no necessity whatever for admitting, with Biot, Lassen and others, that the Hindus went to China to gain their simplest elementary notions of lunar chrononomy. First of all, the Chinese began with twenty-four, and raised them to twenty-eight; the Hindus began with twenty-seven, and raised them to twenty-eight. Secondly, out of these twenty eight asterisms, there are seventeen only which can really be identified with the Hindu stars. Now if a scientific system is borrowed, it is borrowed complete. But, in our case, I see really no possible channel through which Chinese astronomical knowledge could have been conducted to India so early as 1,000 before our era. In Chinese literature India is never mentioned before the middle of the second century before Christ; and if the Chinas in the later Sanskrit literature are meant for Chinese, which is doubtful, it is important to observe that name never occurs in Vedic literature.

When therefore the impossibility of so early a communication between China and India had at last been recognised, a new theory was formed, namely, 'that the knowledge of Chinese astronomy was not imported straight from China to India, but was carried, together with the Chinese system of division of the heavens into twenty-eight mansions, into Western Asia, at a period not much later than 1100

BC, and was then adopted by some Western people, either Semitic or Iranian. In their hands it was supposed to have received a new form, such as adapted it to a ruder and less scientific method of observation, the limiting stars of the mansions being converted into zodiacal groups or constellations, and in some instances altered in position, so as to be brought nearer to the general planetary path of the ecliptic. In this changed form, having become a means of roughly determining and describing the places and movements of the planets, it was believed to have passed into the keeping of the Hindus, very probably along with the first knowledge of the planets themselves, and entered upon an independent career of history in India. It still maintained itself in its old seat, leaving its traces later in the *Bundahish*; and made its way so far westward as finally to become known and adopted by the Arabs.' With due respect for the astronomical knowledge of those who hold this view, all I can say is that this is a novel, and nothing but a novel, without any facts to support it, and that the few facts which are known to us do not enable a careful reasoner to go beyond the conclusions stated many years ago by Colebrooke, that the 'Hindus had undoubtedly made some progress at an early period in the astronomy cultivated by them for the regulation of time. Their calendar, both civil and religious, was governed chiefly, not exclusively, by the moon and the sun: and the motions of these luminaries were carefully observed by them, and with such success, that their determination of the moon's synodical revolution, which was what they were principally concerned with, is a much more correct one than the Greeks ever achieved. They had a division of the ecliptic into twenty-seven and twenty-eight parts, suggested evidently by the moon's period in days, and seemingly their own; it was certainly borrowed by the Arabians.'

There is one more argument which has been adduced in support of a Babylonian, or, at all events, a Semitic influence to be discovered in Vedic literature which we must shortly examine. It refers to the story of the deluge.

That story, as you know, has been traced in the traditions of many races, which could not well have borrowed it from one another; and it was rather a surprise that no allusion even to a local deluge should occur in any of the Vedic hymns, particularly as very elaborate accounts of different kinds of deluges are found in the later Epic poems, and in the still later Puranas, and form in fact a very familiar subject in the religious traditions of the people of India.

Three of the *Avataras* or incarnations of Vishnu are connected with a deluge, that of the *Fish*, that of the *Tortoise*, and that of the *Boar*, Vishnu in each case rescuing mankind from destruction by water, by assuming the form of a fish, or a tortoise, or a boar.

This being so, it seemed a very natural conclusion to make that, as there was no mention of a deluge in the most ancient literature of India, that legend had penetrated into India from without at a later time.

When, however, the Vedic literature became more generally known, stories of a deluge were discovered, if not in the hymns, at least, in the prose writings, belonging to the second period, commonly called the Brahmana period. Not only the story of Manu and the *Fish*, but the stories of the *Tortoise* and of the *Boar* also, were met with there in a more or less complete form, and with this discovery the idea of a foreign importation lost much of its plausibility. I shall read you at least one of these accounts of a deluge which is found in the *Satapatha Brahmana*, and you can then judge for yourselves whether the similarities between it and the account in *Genesis* are really such as to require, nay as to admit, the hypothesis that the Hindus borrowed their account of the deluge from their nearest Semitic neighbours.

We read in the *Satapatha Brahmana*, I.8.1:

'In the morning they brought water to Manu for washing, as they bring it even now for washing our hands.

'While he was thus washing, a fish came into his hands.

'2. The fish spoke this word to Manu: "Keep me, and I shall save thee."

'Manu said: "From what wilt thou save me?"

'The fish said: "A flood will carry away all these creatures, and I shall save thee from it."

'Manu said: "How canst thou be kept?"

'3. The fish said: "So long as we are small, there is much destruction for us, for fish swallows fish. Keep me therefore first in a jar. When I outgrow that, dig a hole and keep me in it. When I outgrow that, take me to the sea, and I shall then be beyond the reach of destruction."

'4. He became soon a large fish, for such a fish grows largest. The fish said: "In such and such a year the flood will come. Therefore when thou hast built a ship, thou shalt meditate on me. And when the flood has risen, thou shalt enter into the ship, and I will save thee from the flood."

'5. Having thus kept the fish, Manu took him to the sea. Then in the same year which the fish had pointed out, Manu, having built the ship, meditated on the fish. And when the flood had risen, Manu entered into the ship. Then the fish swam towards him, and Manu fastened the rope of the ship to the fish's horn, and he thus hastened towards the Northern Mountain.

'6. The fish said: "I have saved thee; bind the ship to a tree. May the water not cut thee off; while thou art on the mountain. As the water subsides, do thou gradually slide down with it." Manu then slid down gradually with the water, and therefore this is called "the Slope of Manu" on the Northern Mountain. Now the flood had carried away all these creatures, and thus Manu was left there alone.

'7. Then Manu went about singing praises and toiling, wishing for offspring. And he sacrificed there also with a Paka-sacrifice. He poured clarified butter, thickened milk, whey, and curds in the water as a libation. In one year a woman arose from it. She came forth as if dripping, and clarified butter gathered on her step. Mitra and Varuna came to meet her.

'8. They said to her: "Who art thou?" She said: "The daughter of Manu." They rejoined: "Say that thou art ours.". "No," she said, "he who has begotten me, his I am."

'Then they wished her to be their sister, and she half agreed and half did not agree, but went away, and came to Manu.

'9. Manu said to her: "Who art thou?" She said: "I am thy daughter." "How, lady, art thou my daughter?" he asked.

'She replied: "The libations which thou hast poured into the water, clarified butter, thickened milk, whey and curds, by them thou hast begotten me. I am a benediction—perform this benediction at the sacrifices. If thou perform it at the sacrifice, thou wilt be rich in offspring and cattle. And whatever blessing thou wilt ask by me, will always accrue to thee." He therefore performed that benediction in the middle of the sacrifice, for the middle of the sacrifice is that which comes between the introductory and the final offerings.

'10. Then Manu went about with her, singing praises and toiling, wishing for offspring. And with her he begat that offspring which is called the offspring of Manu; and whatever blessing he asked with her, always accrued to him. She is indeed Ida, and whosoever, knowing this, goes about (sacrifices) with Ida, begets the same offspring which Manu begat, and whatever blessing he asks with her, always accrues to him.'

This, no doubt, is the account of a deluge, and Manu acts in some respects the same part which is assigned to Noah in the *Old Testament*. But if there are similarities, think of the dissimilarities, and how they are to be explained. It is quite clear that, if this story was borrowed from a Semitic source, it was not borrowed from the *Old Testament*, for in that ease it would really seem impossible to account for the differences between the two stories. That it may have been borrowed from some unknown Semitic source cannot, of course, be disproved, because no tangible proof has ever been produced that would admit of being disproved. But if it were, it would be the only Semitic loan in ancient Sanskrit literature—and that ought to make us pause!

The story of the board and the tortoise too, can be traced back to the Vedic literature. For we read in the *Tattiriya Samhita*:

'At first this was water, fluid. Prajapati, the lord of creatures, having become wind, moved on it. He saw this earth, and becoming a boar, he took it up. Becoming Visvakarman, the maker of all things, he cleaned it. It spread and became the wide-spread earth, and this is why the earth is called Prithivi, the wide-spread.'

And we find in the *Satapatha Brahmana* the following slight allusion at least to the tortoise myth:

'Prajapati, assuming the form of a tortoise brought forth all creatures. In so far as he brought them forth, he made them, and because he made them he was (called) tortoise (Kurma). A tortoise is (called) Kasyapa, and therefore all creatures are called Kasyapa, tortoise-like. He who was this tortoise was really Aditya, (the sun).'

One other allusion to something like a deluge, important chiefly on account of the name of Manu occurring in it, has been pointed out in the *Kathaka* where this short sentence occurs: 'The waters cleaned this. Manu alone remained.'

All this shows that ideas of a deluge, that is, of a submersion of the earth by water and of its rescue through divine aid, were not altogether unknown in the early traditions of India, while in later times they were embodied in several of the *avataras* of Vishnu.

When we examine the numerous accounts of a deluge among different nations in almost every part of the world, we can easily perceive that they do not refer to one single historical event, but to a natural phenomenon repeated every year, namely the deluge or food of the rainy season or the winter.

If that is so, we have surely a right to claim the same natural origin for the story of the deluge in India which we are bound to admit in other countries. And even if it could be proved that in the form in which these legends have reached us in India they show traces of foreign influences, the fact would still remain that such influences have been perceived in comparatively modern treatises only, and not in the ancient hymns of the *Rigveda*.

Other conjectures have been made with even less foundation than that which would place the ancient poets of India under the influence of Babylon. China has been appealed to, ray even Persia. Parthia, and Bactria, countries beyond the reach of India at that early time of which we are here speaking. I only wonder that traces of the lost Jewish tribes have not been discovered in the Vedas, considering that Afghanistan has so often been pointed out as one of their favourite retreats.

After having thus carefully examined all the traces of supposed foreign influences that have been brought forward by various scholars. I think I may say that there really is no trace whatever of any foreign influence in the language, the religion, or the ceremonial of the ancient Vedic literature of India. As it stands before us now, so it has grown up, protected by the mountain ramparts in the North, the Indus and the desert in the West, the Indus or what was called the sea in the South, and the Ganges in the East. It presents us with a home-grown poetry, and a home-grown religion; and history has preserved to us at least this one relic, in order to teach us what the human mind can achieved if left to itself, surrounded by a scenery and by conditions of life that might have made man's life on earth a paradise, if man did not possess the strange art of turning even a paradise into a place of misery.

NOTES

Pages

76. **di color che sanno:** the caste (*varna*) of those who know.

79. **Cardinal Manning** (1808-92): An Anglican prelate who joined the Roman Catholic Church, an ecclesiastical statesman and controversialist.
Comte (August, 1789-1857): French mathematician and philosopher, the founder of Positivism, a system of thought which excludes metaphysics and revealed religion, and substitutes the Religion of Humanity.

82. **the five mahayajnas:** See pp. 143-44 below.
Agnihotra: oblation to fire (*agni*).

84. **Biot:** (Edouard-Constant 1803-50): French Sinologist.
Lassen: (Christian, 1800-76): German Orientalist; author of an extensive treatise on Indian archaeology.

85. **Bundahish:** Sacred book of the Parsis, written in Pehlevi. Though composed in the 3rd century AD, this work contains doctrines of very ancient origin, and forms a supplement to the *Zend-Avesta.*
86. **Avataras:** ten, of which those of Rama and Krishna are the best known.
87. **Paka:** cooked food.
offspring of Manu: Manava, man.
Ida: Name of this woman, born of Manu, and of the sacrificial cake. The whole story is an instance of euhemerism, so common in the Brahmanas.
88. **Noah in the Old Testament:** *Genesis,* chs. VI-IX.
Kurma: an attempt to connect the name of the tortoise with the root of *kuru,* meaning 'do' or 'make.'

LECTURE V

The Religion of The Veda

ALTHOUGH there is hardly any department of learning which has not received new light and new life from the ancient literature of India, yet nowhere is the light that comes to us from India so important, so novel, and so rich as in the study of religion and mythology. It is to this subject therefore that I mean to devote the remaining lectures of this course. I do so, partly because I feel myself most at home in that ancient world of Vedic literature in which the germs of Aryan religion have to be studied, partly because I believe that for a proper understanding of the deepest convictions, or, if you like, the strongest prejudices of the modern Hindus, nothing is so useful as a knowledge of the Veda. It is perfectly true that nothing would give a falser impression of the present Brahmanical religion than the ancient Vedic literature, supposing we were to imagine that three thousand years could have passed over India without producing any change. Such a mistake would be nearly as absurd as to deny any difference between the Vedic Sanskrit and the spoken Bengali. But no one will gain a scholar like knowledge or a true insight into the secret springs of Bengali who is ignorant of the grammar of Sanskrit; and no one will ever understand the present religious, philosophical, legal, and social opinions of the Hindus, who is unable to trace them back to their true sources in the Veda.

I still remember how, many years ago, when I began to publish for the first time the text and the commentary of the *Rigveda*, it was argued by a certain, perhaps not quite disinterested party, that the Veda was perfectly useless, that no man in India, however learned, could read it, and that it was of no use either for missionaries or for any one else who wished to study and to influence the native mind. It was said that we ought to study the later Sanskrit, the Laws of Manu, the epic poems, and, more particularly, the Puranas. The Veda might do very well for German students, but not for Englishmen.

There was no excuse for such ignorant assertions even thirty years ago, for in these very books, in the Laws of Manu, in the *Mahabharata*, and in the Puranas, the Veda is everywhere proclaimed as the highest authority in all matters of religion. 'A Brahman,' says Manu, 'unlearned in holy writ, is extinguished in an instant like dry grass on fire.' 'A twice-born man (that is a Brahmana, a Kshatriya, and a Vaisya) not having studied the Veda, soon falls, even when living, to the condition of a Sudra, and his descendants after him.'

How far this license of ignorant assertion may be carried is shown by the same authorities who denied the importance of the Veda for a historical study of Indian thought, boldly charging those wily priests, the Brahmans, with having withheld their sacred literature from any but their own caste. Now so far from withholding it, the Brahmans have always been striving, and often striving in vain, to make the study of their sacred literature obligatory on all castes, except the Sudras, and the passages just quoted from Manu show what penalties were threatened, if children of the second and third castes, the Kshatriyas and Vaisyas, were not instructed in the sacred literature of the Brahmans.

At present the Brahmans themselves have spoken, and the reception they have accorded to my edition of the *Rigveda* and its native commentary, the zeal with which they have themselves taken up the study of Vedic literature, and the earnestness with which different sects are still discussing the proper use that should be made of their ancient religious writings, show abundantly that a Sanskrit scholar ignorant of or, I should rather say, determined to ignore the Veda, would be not much better than a Hebrew scholar ignorant of the *Old Testament*.

I shall now proceed to give you some characteristic specimens of the religion and poetry on the *Rigveda*. They can only be few, and as there is nothing like system on unity of plan in that collection of 1017 hymns, which we call the Samhita of the *Rigveda*, I cannot promise that they will give you a complete panoramic view of that intellectual world in which our Vedic ancestors passed their life on earth.

I could not even answer the question, if you were to ask it, whether the religion of the Veda was *polytheistic*, or *monotheistic*. Monotheistic, in the usual sense of that word, it is decidedly not, though there are hymns that assert the unity of the Divine as fearlessly as any passage of the *Old Testament*, or the *New Testament*, or the *Koran*. Thus one poet says: 'That which is *one*, sages name it in various ways—they call it Agni, Yama, Matarisvan.'

Another poet says: 'The wise poets represent by their words Him who is one with beautiful wings, in many ways.'

And again we hear of a being called Hiranyagarbha, the golden germ (whatever the original of that name may have been), of whom the poet says: 'In the beginning there arose Hiranyagarbha; he was the one born lord of all this. He established the earth and this sky. Who is the god to whom we shall offer our sacrifice?' That Hiranyagarbha, the poet says, 'is alone God above all gods'—an assertion of the unity of the Divine which could hardly be exceeded in strength by any passage from the *Old Testament*.

But by the side of such passages, which are few in number, there are thousands in which ever so many divine beings are praised and prayed to. Their number is sometimes given as 'thrice eleven' or thirty-three, and one poet assigns eleven gods to the sky, eleven to the earth, and eleven to the waters, the waters here intended being those of the atmosphere and the clouds. These thirty-three gods have even wives apportioned to them, though few of these only have as yet attained to the honour of a name.

These thirty-three gods, however, by no means include all the Vedic gods, for such important deities as Agni, the fire, Soma, the rain, the Maruts or storm-gods, the Asvins, the gods of morning and evening, the waters, the dawn, the sun, are mentioned separately; and there are not wanting passages in which the poet is carried away into exaggerations, till he proclaims the number of his gods to be, not only thirty-three, but three thousand three hundred and thirty-nine.

If therefore there must be a name for the religion of the *Rigveda*, polytheism would seem at first sight the most appropriate. Polytheism, however, has assumed with us a meaning which renders it totally inapplicable to the Vedic religion.

Our ideas of polytheism being chiefly derived from Greece and Rome, we understand by it a certain more or less organised system of gods, different in power and rank and all subordinate to a supreme God, a Zeus or Jupiter. The Vedic polytheism differs from the Greek and Roman polytheism, and, I may add, likewise from the polytheism of the Ural-Altaic, the Polynesian, the American, and most of the African races, in the same manner as a confederacy of village communities differs from a monarchy. There are traces of an earlier stage of village-community life to be discovered in the later republican and monarchical constitutions, and in the same manner nothing can be clearer, particularly in Greece, than that the monarchy of Zeus was preceded by what may be called the septarchy of several of the great gods of Greece. The same remark applies to the mythology of the Teutonic nations also. In the Veda, however, the gods worshipped as supreme by each sept stand still side by side. No one is first always, no one is last always. Even gods of a decidedly inferior and limited character assume occasionally in the eyes of a devoted poet a supreme place above all other gods. It was necessary, therefore, for the purpose of accurate reasoning to have a name, different from polytheism, to signify this worship of single gods, each occupying for a time a supreme position, and I proposed for it the name of Kathenotheism, that is a worship of one god after another, or of henotheism, the worship of single gods. This shorter name of henotheism has found more general acceptance, as conveying more definitely the opposition between monotheism, the worship of one only God, and henotheism, the worship of single gods; and, if but properly defined, it will answer its purpose very well. However, in researches of this kind we cannot be too much on our guard against technical terms. They are inevitable, I know; but they are almost always misleading. There is, for instance, a hymn addressed to the Indus and the rivers that fall into it, of which I hope to read you a translation, because it determines very accurately the geographical scene on which the poets of the Veda passed their life. Native scholars call these rivers *devatas* or deities, and European translators too speak of them as gods and goddesses. But in the language used by the poet with regard to the Indus and the other rivers, there is nothing to justify us in saying that he considered these rivers as gods and goddesses, unless we mean by gods and goddesses something very different from what the Greeks called River-gods and River-goddesses, Nymphs, Najades, or even Muses.

And what applies to these rivers, applies more or less to all the objects of Vedic worship. They all are still oscillating between what is seen by the senses, what is created by fancy, and what is postulated by the understanding; they are things, persons, causes, according to the varying disposition of the poets: and if we call them gods or goddesses, we must remember the remark of an ancient native theologian, who reminds us that *by devata* or deity he means no more than the object celebrated in a hymn, while *rishi* or seer means no more than the subject or the author of a hymn.

It is difficult to treat of the so-called gods celebrated in the Veda according to any system, for the simple reason that the concepts of these gods and the hymns addressed to them sprang up spontaneously and without any pre-established plan. It is best perhaps for our purpose to follow an ancient Brahmanical writer, who is supposed to have lived about 400 BC. He tells us of students of the Veda, before his time, who admitted three deities only, viz. Agni or fire, whose place is on the earth; Vayu or Indra, the wind and the god of the thunderstorm, whose place is in the air; and Surya, the sun, whose place is in the sky. These deities, they maintained, received severally many appellations, in consequence of their greatness, or of the diversity of their functions; just as a priest, according to the functions which he performs at various sacrifices, receives various names.

This is *one* view of the Vedic gods, and, though too narrow, it cannot be denied that there is some truth in it. A very useful division of the Vedic gods might be made, and has been made by Yaska, into *terrestrial, aerial,* and *celestial,* and if the old Hindu theologian meant no more than that all the manifestations of divine power in nature might be traced back to three centres of force, one in the sky, one in the air, and one on the earth, he deserves great credit for his sagacity.

But he himself perceived evidently that his generalisation was not quite applicable to all the gods, and he goes on to say, 'Or, it may be, these gods are all distinct beings, for the praises addressed to them are distinct, and their appellations also.' This is quite right. It is the very object of most of these divine names to impart distinct individuality to the manifestations of the powers of nature; and thougn the philosopher or the inspired poet might perceive that these numerous names were but names, while that which was named was *one* and *one* only, this was certainly not the idea of most of the Vedic *rishis* themselves, still less of the people who listened to their songs at fairs and festivals. It is the peculiar character of that phase of religious thought which we have to study in the Veda, that in it the Divine is conceived and represented as manifold, and that many functions are shared in common by various gods, no attempt having yet been made at organising the whole body of the gods, sharply separating one from the other, and subordinating all of them to several or, in the end, to one supreme head.

Availing ourselves of the division of the Vedic gods into terrestrial, aerial, and celestial, as proposed by some of the earliest Indian theologians, we should have to begin with the gods connected with the earth.

Before we examine them, however, we have first to consider one of the earliest objects of worship and adoration, namely earth and heaven, or heaven and earth, conceived as a divine couple. Not only in India, but among many other nations, both savage, half-savage, or civilized, we meet with Heaven and Earth as one of the earliest objects, pondered on, transfigured, and animated by the early poets, and more or less clearly conceived by early philosophers. It is surprising that it should be so, for the conception of the earth as an independent being, and of heaven as an independent being, and then of both together as a divine couple embracing the whole universe, requires a considerable effort of abstraction, far more than the concepts of their divine powers, such as the fire, the rain, the lightning, or the sun.

Still so it is, and as it may help us to understand the ideas about heaven and earth, as we find them in the Veda, and show us at the same time the strong contrast between the mythology of the Aryans and that of real savages (a contrast of great importance, though I admit very difficult to explain), I shall read you first some extracts from a book, published by a friend of mine, the Rev. William Wyatt Gill, for many years an active and most successful missionary in Mangaia, one of those Polynesian islands that form a girdle round one quarter of our globe, and all share in the same language, the same religion, the same mythology, and the same customs. The book is called *Myths and Songs from the South Pacific,* and it is full of interest to the student of mythology and religion.

The story, as told him by the natives of Mangaia, runs as follows:

The sky is built of solid blue stone. At one time it almost touched the earth; resting upon the stout broad leaves of the teve (which attains the height of about six feet) and the delicate indigenous arrow-root (whose slender stem rarely exceeds three feet) .... In this narrow space between earth and sky the inhabitants of this world were pent up. Ru, whose usual residence was in Avaiki, or the shades, had come up for a time to this world of ours. Pitying the wretched confined residence of the inhabitants, he employed himself in endeavouring to raise the sky a little. For this purpose he cut a number of strong stakes of different kinds of trees, and firmly planted them in the ground at Rangimotia, the centre of the island,

and with him the centre of the world. This was a considerable improvement, as mortals were thereby enabled to stand erect and to walk about without inconvenience. Hence Ru was named "The sky-supporter." Wherefore Teka sings (1794):

"Force up the sky, O Ru,
And let the space be clear!"

'One day when the old man was surveying his work, his graceless son Maui contemptuously asked him what he was doing there. Ru replied, "Who told youngsters to talk? Take care of yourself, or I will hurl you out of existence."

'"Do it, then," shouted Maui.

'Ru was as good as his word, and forthwith seized Maui, who was small of stature, and threw him to a great height. In falling Maui assumed the form of a bird, and lightly touched the ground, perfectly unharmed. Maui, now thirsting for revenge, in a moment resumed his natural form, but exaggerated to gigantic proportions, and ran to his father, saying:

"Ru, who supportest the many heavens,
The third, even to the highest, ascend!"

Inserting his head between the old man's legs, he exerted all his prodigious strength, and hurled poor Ru, sky and all, to a tremendous height,—so high, indeed, that the blue sky could never get back again. Unluckily, however, for the sky-supporting Ru, his head and shoulders got entangled among the stars. He struggled hard, but fruitlessly, to extricate himself. Maui walked off well pleased with having raised the sky to its present height, but left half his father's body and both his legs ingloriously suspended between heaven and earth. Thus perished Ru. His body rotted away, and his bones came tumbling down from time to time, and were shivered on the earth into countless fragments. These shivered bones of Ru are scattered over every hill and valley of Mangaia, to the very edge of the sea.'

What the natives call the 'bones of Ru' are pieces of pumice-stone.

Now let us consider, first of all, whether this story, which with slight variations in told all over the Polynesian islands, is pure non-sense, or whether there was originally some sense in it. My conviction is that non-sense is everywhere the child of sense, only that unfortunately many children, like that youngster Maui, consider themselves much wiser than their fathers, and occasionally succeed in hurling them out of existence.

It is a peculiarity of many of the ancient myths that they represent events, which happen every day, or every year, as having happened once upon a time. The daily battle between day and night, the yearly battle between winter and spring, are represented almost like historical events, and some of the episodes and touches belonging originally to these constant battles of nature, have certainly been transferred into and mixed up with battles that took place at a certain time, such as, for instance, the siege of Troy. When historical recollections failed, legendary accounts of the ancient battles between night and morning, winter and spring, were always at hand; and, as in modern times we constantly hear 'good stories,' which we have known from our childhood, told again and again of any man whom they seem to fit, in the same manner, in ancient times, any act of prowess, or daring, or mischief, originally told of the sun, 'the orient Conqueror of gloomy Night,' was readily transferred to and believed of any local hero who might seem to be a second Jupiter, or Mars, or Hercules.

I have little doubt therefore that as the accounts of a deluge, for instance, which we find almost everywhere, are originally recollections of the annual torrents of rain or snow that covered the little worlds within the ken of the ancient village-bards, this tearing asunder of heaven and earth too was originally no more than a description of what might be seen every morning. During a dark night the sky seemed to cover the earth; the two seemed to be one, and could not be distinguished one from the other. Then came the dawn, which with its bright rays lifted the covering of the dark night to a certain point, till at last Maui appeared, small in stature, a mere child, that is, the sun of the morning—thrown up suddenly, as it were, when his first rays shot through the sky from beneath the horizon, then falling back to the earth, like a bird, and rising in gigantic form on the morning sky. The dawn now was hurled away, and the sky was seen lifted high above the earth; and Maui, the sun, marched on well pleased with having raised the sky to its present height.

Why pumice-stone should be called the bones of Ru, we cannot tell, without knowing a great deal more of the language of Mangaia than we do at present. It is most likely an independent saying, and was afterwards united with the story of Ru and Maui.

Now I must quote at least a few extracts from a Maori legend as written down by Judge Manning:

'This is the *Genesis* of the New Zealanders:

'The Heavens which are above us, and the Earth which lies beneath us, are the progenitors of men, and the origin of all things.

'Formerly the Heaven lay upon the Earth, and all was darkness ....

'And the children of Heaven and Earth sought to discover the difference between light and darkness, between day and night. . . .

'So the sons of Rangi (Heaven) and of Papa (Earth) consulted together, and said: "Let us seek means whereby to destroy Heaven and Earth, or to separate them from each other,"

'Then said Tumatauenga (the God of War), "Let us destroy them both."

'Then said Tane-Mahuta (the Forest God), "Not so; let them be separated. Let one of them go upwards and become a stranger to us; let the other remain below and be a parent for us."

'Then four of the gods tried to separate Heaven and Earth, but did not succeed, while the fifth, Tane, succeeded.

'After Heaven and Earth had been separated, great storms arose, or, as the poet expresses it, one of their sons, Tawhiri-Matea, the god of the winds, tried to revenge the outrage committed on his parents by his brothers. Then follow dismal dusky days, and dripping chilly skies, and arid scorching blasts. All the gods fight, till at last Tu only remains, the god of war, who had devoured all his brothers, except the Storm. More fights follow, in which the greater part of the earth was overwhelmed by the waters, and but a small portion remained dry. After that, light continued to increase, and as the light increased, so also the people who had been hidden between Heaven and Earth increased. . . . And so generation was added to generation down to the time of Maui-Potiki, he who brought death into the world.

'Now in these latter days Heaven remains far removed from his wife, the Earth; but the love of the wife rises upward in sighs towards her husband. These are the mists which fly upwards from the mountain-tops; and the tears of Heaven fall downwards on his wife; behold the dew-drops!'

So far the Maori *Genesis.*

Let us now return to the Veda, and compare these crude and somewhat grotesque legends with the language of the ancient Aryan poets. In the hymns of the *Rigveda* the separating and keeping apart of heaven and earth is several times alluded to, and here too it is represented as the work of the most valiant gods. In I.67.3 it is Agni, fire, who holds the earth and supports the heaven; in X.89.4 it is Indra who keeps them apart; in IX.101.15 Soma is celebrated for the same deed, and in III.31.12 other gods too share the same honour.

In the *Aitareya Brahmana* we read: 'These two worlds (Heaven and Earth) were once joined together. They went asunder. Then it did not rain, nor did the sun shine. And the five tribes did not agree with one another. The gods then brought the two (Heaven and Earth) together, and when they came together, they performed a wedding of the gods.'

Here we have in a shorter form the same fundamental ideas; first, that formerly heaven and earth were together; that afterwards they were separated; that when they were thus separated there was war throughout nature, and neither rain nor sunshine; that, lastly, heaven and earth were conciliated, and that then a great wedding took place.

Now I need hardly remind those who are acquainted with Greek and Roman literature, how familiar these and similar conceptions about a marriage between heaven and earth were in Greece and Italy. They seem to possess there a more special reference to the annual reconciliation between heaven and earth, which takes place in spring, and to their former estrangement during winter. But the first cosmological separation of the two always points to the want of light and the impossibility of distinction during the night, and the gradual lifting up of the blue sky through the rising of the sun.

In the Homeric hymns the earth is addressed as:

'Mother of gods, the wife of the starry Heaven;'

and the Heaven or Æther is often called the father. Their marriage too is described, as, for instance, by Euripides, when he says:

'There is the mighty Earth, Jove's Æther:
He (the Æther is the creator of men and gods;
The earth receiving the moist drops of rain,
Bears mortals,
Bears food, and the tribes of animals,
Hence she is not unjustly regarded
As the mother of all.'

And what is more curious still is that we have evidence that Euripides received this doctrine from his teacher, the philosopher

Anaxagoras. For Dionysius of Halicarnassus tells us that Euripides frequented the lectures of Anaxagoras. Now, it was the theory of that philosopher that originally all things were in all things, but that afterwards they became separated. Euripides later in life associated with Socrates, and became doubtful regarding that theory. He accordingly propounds the ancient doctrine by the mouth of another, namely Melanippe, who says:

'This saying (myth) is not mine, but came from my mother, that formerly Heaven and Earth were one shape; but when they were separated from each other, they gave birth and brought all things into the light, trees, birds, beasts, and the fishes whom the sea feeds, and the race of mortals.'

Thus we have met with the same idea of the original union, of a separation, and of a subsequent reunion of heaven and earth in Greece, in India, and in the Polynesian islands.

Let us now see how the poets of the Veda address these two beings, heaven and earth.

They are mostly addressed in the dual, as two beings forming but one concept. We meet, however, with verses which are addressed to the earth by herself, and which speak of her as 'kind without thorns, and pleasant to dwell on,' while there are clear traces in some of the hymns that at one time Dyaus, the sky, was the supreme deity. When invoked together they are called Dyavaprithivyau, from *dyu*, the sky, and Prithivi, the broad earth.

If we examine their epithets, we find that many of them reflect simply the physical aspects of heaven and earth. Thus they are called *uru*, wide, *uruvyachas*, widely expanded, *dure-ante*, with limits far apart, *gabhira*, deep, *ghritavat*, giving fat, *madhudugha*, yielding honey or dew, *payasvat*, full of milk, *bhuri-retas*, rich in seed.

Another class of epithets represents them already as endowed with certain human and superhuman qualities, such as *asaschat*, never tiring, *ajara*, not decaying, which brings us very near to immortal; *adruh*, not injuring, or not deceiving, *prachetas*, provident, and then *pita-mata*, father and mother, *devaputra*; having the gods for their sons, *ritavridh* and *ritavat*, protectors of the Rita, of what is right, guardians of eternal laws.

Here you see what is so interesting in the Veda, the gradual advance from the material to the spiritual, from the sensuous to the supersensuous, from the human to the superhuman and the divine. Heaven and earth were seen, and, according to our notions, they might simply be classed as visible and finite beings. But the ancient poets were more honest to themselves. They could see heaven and earth, but they never saw them in their entirety. They felt that there was something beyond the purely finite aspect of these beings, and therefore they thought of them, not as they would think of a stone, or a tree, or a dog, but as something not-finite, not altogether visible or knowable, yet as something important to themselves, powerful, strong to bless, but also strong to hurt. Whatever was between heaven and earth seemed to be theirs, their property, their realm, their dominion. They held and embraced all; they seemed to have produced all. The Devas or bright beings, the sun, the dawn, the fire, the wind, the rain, were all theirs and were called therefore the offspring of heaven and earth. Thus heaven and earth became the universal father and mother.

Then we ask at once, 'Were then these heaven and earth gods? But gods in what sense? In our sense of God? Why, in our sense, God is altogether incapable of a plural. Then in the Greek sense of the word? No, certainly not, for what the Greeks called gods was the result of an intellectual growth totally independent of the Veda or of India. We must never forget that what we call gods in ancient mythologies are not substantial, living, individual beings, of whom we can predicate this or that. Deva, which we translate by god, was originally nothing but an adjective, expressive of a quality shared by heaven and earth, by the sun and the stars and the dawn and the sea, namely *brightness*; and the idea of god, at that early time, contains neither more nor less than what is shared in common by all these bright beings. That is to say, the idea of God is not an idea readymade, which could be applied in its abstract purity to heaven and earth and other such-like beings; but it is an idea, growing out of the concepts of heaven and earth and of the other bright beings, slowly separating itself from them, but never containing more than what was contained, though confusedly, in the objects to which it was successively applied.

Nor must it be supposed that heaven and earth, having once been raised to the rank of undecaying or immortal beings, of divine parents, of guardians of the laws, were thus permanently settled in the religious consciousness of the people. Far from it. When the ideas of other gods, and of more active and more distinctly personal gods had been elaborated, the Vedic *rishis* asked without hesitation, who then has made heaven and earth? not exactly heaven and earth, as conceived before, but heaven and earth as seen every day, as a part of what began to be called Nature or the Universe.

Thus one poet says:

'He was indeed among the gods the cleverest workman who produced the two brilliant ones (heaven and earth), that gladden all things; he who measured out the two bright ones (heaven and earth) by his wisdom, and established them on everlasting supports.'

And again: 'He was a good workman who produced heaven and earth; the wise, who by his might brought together these two (heaven and earth), the wide, the deep, the well-fashioned in bottomless space.'

Very soon this great work of making heaven and earth was ascribed, like other mighty works, to the mightiest of their gods, to Indra. At first we read that Indra, originally only a kind of Jupiter pluvius, or god of rain, stretched out heaven and earth, like a hide; that he held them in his hand, that he upholds heaven and earth, and that he grants heaven and earth to his worshippers. But very soon Indra is praised for having made heaven and earth; and then, when the poet remembers that heaven and earth had been praised elsewhere as the parents of the gods, and more especially as the parent of Indra, he does not hesitate for a moment, but says: 'What poets living before us have reached the end of all thy greatness? for thou hast indeed begotten thy father and thy mother together from thy own body!'

That is a strong measure, and a god who once could do that, was no doubt capable of anything afterwards. The same idea, namely that Indra is greater than heaven and earth, is expressed in a less outrageous way by another poet, who says that Indra is greater than heaven and earth, and that both together are only a half of Indra. Or again: 'The divine Dyaus bowed before Indra, before Indra the great earth bowed with her wide spaces.' 'At the birth of thy splendour Dyaus trembled, the earth trembled for fear of thy anger.'

Thus, from one point of view, heaven and earth were the greatest gods, they were the parents of everything, and therefore of the gods also, such as Indra and others.

But, from another point of view, every god that was considered as supreme at one time or other, must necessarily have made heaven and earth, must at all events be greater than heaven and earth, and thus the child became greater than the father, aye, became the father of his father. Indra was not the only god that created heaven and earth. In one hymn that creation is ascribed to Soma and Pushan, by no means very prominent characters; in another to Hiranyagarbha (the golden germ); in another again, to a god who is simply called Dhatri, the Creator, or Visvakarman, the maker of all things. Other gods, such as Mitra and Savitri, names of the sun, are praised for upholding heaven and earth, and the same task is sometimes performed by the old god Varuna also.

What I wish you to observe in all this is the perfect freedom with which these so-called gods or Devas are handled, and particularly the ease and naturalness with which now the one, now the other emerges as supreme out of this chaotic theogony. This is the peculiar character of the ancient Vedic religion, totally different both from the polytheism and from the monotheism as we see it in the Greek and the Jewish religions; and if the Veda had taught us nothing else but this henotheistic phase, which must everywhere have preceded the more highly organised phase of polytheism which we see in Greece, in Rome, and elsewhere, the study of the Veda would not have been in vain.

It may be quite true that the poetry of the Veda is neither beautiful, in our sense of the word, nor very profound; but it is instructive. When we see those two giant spectres of heaven and earth on the background of the Vedic religion, exerting their influence for a time, and then vanishing before the light of younger and more active gods, we learn a lesson which it is well to learn, and which we can hardly learn anywhere else—the lesson *how gods were made and unmade*—how the Beyond or the Infinite was named by different names in order to bring it near to the mind of man, to make it for a time comprehensive, until, when name after name had proved of no avail, a nameless God was felt to answer best the restless cravings of the human heart.

I shall next translate to you the hymn to which I referred before as addressed to the rivers. It the rivers are to be called deities at all, they belong to the class of terrestrial deities. But the reason why I single out this hymn is not so much because it throws new light on the theogonic process, but because it may help to impart some reality to the vague conceptions which we form to ourselves of the ancient Vedic poets and their surroundings. The rivers invoked are, as we shall see, the real rivers of the Punjab, and the poem shows a much wider geographical horizon than we should expect from a mere village bard.

1. 'Let the poet declare, O Waters, your exceeding greatness, here in the seat of Vivasvat. By seven and seven they have come forth in three courses, but the Sindhu (the Indus) exceeds all the other wandering rivers by her strength.

2. 'Varuna dug out paths for thee to walk on, when thou rannest to the race. Thou proceedest on a precipitous ridge of the earth, when thou art lord in the van of all the moving streams.

3. 'The sound rises up to heaven above the earth; she stirs up with splendour her endless power. As from a cloud, the showers thunder forth, when the Sindhu comes, roaring like a bull.

4. 'To thee O Sindhu, they (the other rivers) come as lowing mother-cows (run) to their young with their milk. Like a king in battle thou leadest the two wings, when thou reachest the front of these down-rushing rivers.

5. 'Accept, O Ganga (Ganges), Yamuna (Jumna), Sarasvati (Sursuti), Sutudri (Sutlej), Parushni (Iravati, Ravi), my praise! With the Asikni (Akesines) listen, O Marudvridha, and with the Vitasta (Hydaspes, Behat); O Arjikiya, listen with the Sushoma.

6. 'First thou goest united with the Trishtama on the journey, with the Susartu, the Rasa (Ramha, Araxes?), and the Sveti,—O Sindhu, with the Kubha (Kophen, Cabul river) to the Gomati (Gomal), with the Mehatnu to the Krumu (Kurrum)—with whom thou proceedest together.

7. 'Sparkling, bright, with mighty splendour she carries the waters across the plains—the unconquered Sindhu, the quickest of the quick, like a beautiful mare—a sight to see.

8. 'Rich in horses, in chariots, in garments, in gold, in wool, and in straw, the Sindhu, handsome and young, clothes herself in sweet flowers.

9. 'The Sindhu has yoked her easy chariot with horses; may she conquer prizes for us in the race. The greatness of her chariot is praised as truly great—the chariot which is irresistible, which has its own glory, and abundant strength.'

This hymn does not sound perhaps very poetical, in our sense of the word; yet if you will try to realise the thoughts of the poet who composed it, you will perceive that it is not without some bold and powerful conceptions.

Take the modern peasants, living in their villages by the side of the Thames, and you must admit that he would be a remarkable man who could bring himself to look on the Thames as a kind of general, riding at the head of many English rivers, and leading them on to a race or a battle. Yet it is easier to travel in England, and to gain a commanding view of the river-system of the country, than it was three thousand years ago to travel over India, even over that part of India which the poet of our hymn commands. He takes in at one swoop three great river-systems, or, as he calls them, three great armies of rivers—those flowing from the North-West into the Indus, those joining it from the North-East, and, in the distance, the Ganges and the Jumnah with their tributaries. Look on the map and you will see how well these three armies are determined; but our poet had no map—he had nothing but high mountains and sharp eyes to carry out his trigonometrical survey. Now I call a man, who for the first time could *see* those three marching armies of rivers, a poet.

The next thing that strikes one in that hymn—if hymn we must call it—is the fact that all these rivers, large and small, have their own proper names. That shows a considerable advance in civilized life, and it proves no small degree of coherence, or what the French call *solidarity*, between the tribes who had taken possession of Northern India. Most settlers call the river on whose banks they settle '*the river.*' Of course there are many names for river. It may be called the runner, the fertiliser, the roarer—or, with a little poetical metaphor, the arrow, the horse, the cow, the father, the mother, the watchman, the child of the mountains. Many rivers had many names in different parts of their course, and it was only when communication between different settlements became more frequent, and a fixed terminology was felt to be a matter of necessity, that the rivers of a country were properly baptised and registered. All this had been gone through in India before our hymn became possible.

And now we have to consider another, to my mind the most startling fact. We here have a number of names of the rivers of India, as they were known to one single poet, say about 1000 BC. We then hear nothing of India till we come to the days of Alexander, and when we look at the names of the Indian rivers, represented as well as they could be by Alexander's companions, mere strangers in India, and by means of a strange language and a strange alphabet, we recognise, without much difficulty, nearly all of the old Vedic names.

In this respect the names of rivers have a great advantage over the names of towns in India. What we now call Dilli or Delhi was in ancient times called Indraprastha, in later times Shahjahanabad. Oude is Ayodhya, but the old name of Saketa is forgotten. The town of Pataliputra, known to the Greeks as Palimbothra, is now called Patna.

Now I can assure you this persistency of the Vedic river names was to my mind something so startling that I often said to myself. This cannot be—there must be something wrong here. I do not wonder so much at the names of the Indus and the Ganges being the same. The Indus was known to early traders, whether by sea or by land. Skylax sailed from the country of the Paktyes, i.e. the Pushtus, as the Afghans still call themselves, down to the mouth of the Indus. That was under Darius Hystaspes (521-486 BC). Even before that time India and the Indians were known by their name, which was derived from Sindhu, the name of their frontier river. The neighbouring tribes who spoke Iranic languages all pronounced, like the Persian, the *s* as an *h*. Thus Sindhu became Hindhu (Hindu), and, as h's were dropped even at that early time, Hindhu became Indu. Thus the river was called Indos, the people Indoi by the Greeks, who first heard of India through the Persians.

Sindhu probably meant originally the divider, keeper, and defender, from *sidh*, to keep off. It was a masculine, before it became a feminine. No more telling name could have been given to a broad river, which guarded peaceful settlers both against the inroads of hostile tribes and the attacks of wild animals. A common name for the ancient settlements of the Aryans in India was 'the Seven Rivers.' But though Sindhu was used as an appellative noun for river in general, it remained throughout the whole history of India the name of its powerful guardian river, the Indus.

In some passages of the *Rigveda* it has been pointed out that Sindhu might better be translated by 'sea,' a change of meaning, if so it can be called, fully explained by the geographical conditions of the country. There are places where people could swim across the Indus, there are others where no eye could tell whether the boundless expanse of water should be called river or sea. The two run into each other, as every sailor knows, and naturally the meaning of Sindhu, river, runs into the meaning of Sindhu, sea.

But besides the two great rivers, the Indus and the Ganges,—in Sanskrit the Ganga, literally the Go-go,—we have the smaller rivers, and many of their names also agree with the names preserved to us by the companions of Alexander.

The Yamuna, the Jumna, was known to Ptolemy as Diamouna, to Pliny as Jomanes, to Arrian, somewhat corrupted as Jobares.

The Sutudri, or, as it was afterwards called, Satadru, meaning 'running in a hundred streams,' was known to Ptolemy as Zadardes or Zaradros; Pliny called it Sydrus; and Megasthenes, too, was probably acquainted with it as Zadardes. In the Veda it formed with the Vipas the frontier of the Punjab, and we hear of fierce battles fought at that time, it may be on the same spot where in 1846 the battle of the Sutledge was fought by Sir Hugh Gough and Sir Henry Hardinge. It was probably on the Vipas (later Vipasa), a north-western tributary of the Sutledge, that Alexander's army turned back. The river was then called Hyphasis; Pliny calls it Hypasis, a very fair approximation to the Vedic Vipas, which means 'unfettered.' Its modern name is Bias or Bejah.

The next river on the west is the Vedic Parushni, better known as Iravati, which Strabo calls Hyarotis, while Arrian gives it a more Greek appearance by calling it Hydraotes. It is the modern Ravi. It was this river which the Ten Kings when attacking the Tritsus under Sudas tried to cross from the west by cutting off its water. But their strategem failed, and they perished in the river (*Rigveda,* VII.18.8-9).

We then come to the Asikni, which means 'black.' That river had another name also, Chandrabhaga, which means 'streak of the moon.' The Greeks, however, pronounced that name Sandarophagos, and this had the unlucky meaning of 'the devourer of Alexander.' Hesychius tells us that in order to avert the bad omen Alexander changed the name of that river into Akesines, which would mean 'the Healer;' but he does not tell, what the Veda tells us, that this name Akesines, was a Greek adaptation of another name of the same river, namely Asikni, which had evidently supplied to Alexander the idea of calling the Asikni Akesines. It is the modern Chinab.

Next to the Akesines we have the Vedic Vitasta, the last of the rivers of the Punjab, changed in Greek into Hydaspes. It was to this river that Alexander retired, before sending his fleet down the Indus and leading his army back to Babylon. It is the modern Behat or Jhelam.

I could identify still more of these Vedic rivers, such as, for instance, the Kubha, the Greek Cophen, the modern Kabul river; but the names which I have traced from the Veda to Alexander, and in many cases from Alexander again to our own time, seem to me sufficient to impress upon us the real and historical character of the Veda. Suppose the Veda were a forgery—suppose at least that it had been put together after the time of Alexander—how could we explain these names? They are names that have mostly a meaning in Sanskrit, they are names corresponding very closely to their Greek corruptions, as pronounced and written down by people who did not know Sanskrit. How is a forgery possible here?

I selected this hymn for two reasons. First, because it shows us the widest geographical horizon of the Vedic poets, confined by the snowy mountains in the North, the Indus and the range of the Suleiman mountains in the West, the Indus or the sea in the South, and the valley of the Jumna and Ganges in the East. Beyond that, the world, though open, was unknown to the Vedic poets. Secondly, because the same hymn gives us also a kind of historical background to the Vedic age. These rivers, as we may see them today, as they were seen by Alexander and his Macedonians, were seen also by the Vedic poets. Here we have an historical continuity—almost living witnesses, to tell us that the people whose songs have been so strangely, aye, you may almost say, so miraculously preserved to us, were real people, lairds with their clans, priests, or rather, servants of their gods, shepherds with their flocks, dotted about on the hills and valleys, with enclosures or palisades here and there, with a few strongholds, too, in case of need—living their short life on earth, as at that time life might be lived by men, without much pushing and crowding and trampling on each other—spring, summer, and winter leading them on from year to year, and the sun in his rising and setting lifting up their thoughts from their meadows and groves which they loved, to a world in the East, from which they had come, or to a world in the West, to which they were gladly hastening on. They had what I call religion, though it was very simple, and hardly reduced as yet to the form of a creed. 'There is a Beyond,' that was all they felt and knew, though they tried, as well as they could, to give names to that Beyond, and thus to change religion into *a* religion. They had not as yet a name for God—certainly not in our sense of the word—or even a general name for the gods; but they invented name after name to enable them to grasp and comprehend by some outward and visible token powers whose presence they felt in nature, though their true and full essence was to them, as it is to us, invisible and incomprehensible.

NOTES

Pages

98. **The two seemed to be one:** See *Sacred Books of the East*, vol. I, p. 249: (The first half is the earth, the second half the heaven, their uniting the rain, the uniter

Parganya.) And so it is when it (Parganya) rains thus strongly, without ceasing, day and night together, then they say also, 'Heaven and earth have come together.'—(M.M.)

100. **Euripides** (480-406 BC): Greek Tragedian. The passage cited in the text is a fragment preserved by another writer.

101. **Anaxagoras:** Greek philosopher, d. 428 BC. He opened the first school of philosophy in Athens, where Pericles, Euripides and Socrates followed his lessons.

Dionysius of Halicarnassus: Greek historian; contemporary of Augustus.

Socrates (468-399 BC): Celebrated Athenian thinker, whose doctrines are preserved in the writings of his pupils, Plato and Xenophon. He was condemned to death by the popular court of Athens on a charge of impiety. His unpopularity was due to his unsparing mockery and exposure of all shams.

Melanippe: The chief character in one of the plays of Euripides, only fragments of which have survived.

105. **the seat of Vivasvat:** Vivasvat is a name of the sun, and the seat or home of Vivasvat can hardly be anything but the earth, as the home of the sun, or, in a more special sense, the place where a sacrifice is offered.—(M.M.)

107. **Skylax:** Persian commander who explored the sea passage to Persia from the mouths of the Indus.

Ptolemy: Greek astronomer and geographer of the second century AD.

108. **Pliny:** Roman author, born AD 23. His *Natural History* is a sort of cyclopaedia in 37 books.

Arrian: Stoic philosopher and historian (Greek) of the 2nd century AD.

Hesychius: (of Miletus), Greek philosopher of Alexandria, 6th century AD; author of a *Universal Chronicle* and *A Dictionary of Literary History*.

Lecture VI

Vedic Deities

The next important phenomenon of nature which was represented in the Veda as a terrestrial deity is fire, in Sanskrit Agni, in Latin ignis. In the worship which is paid to the fire and in the high praises bestowed on Agni we can clearly perceive the traces of a period in the history of man in which not only the most essential comforts of life, but life itself, depended on the knowledge of producing fire. To us fire has become so familiar that we can hardly form an idea of what life would be without it. But how did the ancient dwellers on earth get command and possession of fire? The Vedic poets tell us that fire first came to them from the sky, in the form of lightning, but that it disappeared again, and that then Matarisvan, a being to a certain extent like Prometheus, brought it back and confided it to the safe keeping of the clan of the Bhrigus (Phlegyas). In other poems we hear of the mystery of producing fire by rubbing pieces of wood; and here it is a curious fact that the name of the wood thus used for rubbing is in Sanskrit Pramantha, a word which, as Kuhn has shown, would in Greek come very near to the name of Prometheus. The possession of fire, whether by preserving it as sacred on the hearth, or by producing it at pleasure with the fire-drill, represents an enormous step in early civilization. It enabled people to cook their meat instead of eating it raw; it gave them the power of carrying on their work by night; and in colder climates it really preserved them from being frozen to death. No wonder, therefore, that the fire should have been praised and worshipped as the best and kindest of gods, the only god who had come down from heaven to live on earth, the friend of man, the messenger of the gods, the mediator between gods and men, the immortal among mortals. He, it is said, protects the settlements of the Aryans, and frightens away the black-skinned enemies.

Soon, however, fire was conceived by the Vedic poets under the more general character of light and warmth, and then the presence of Agni was perceived, not only on the hearth and the altar, but in the dawn, in the sun, and in the world beyond the Sun, while at the same time his power was recognised as ripening, or as they called it, as cooking, the fruits of the earth, and as supporting also the warmth and the life of the human body. From that point of view Agni, like other powers, rose to the rank of a Supreme God. He is said to have stretched out heaven and earth—naturally, because without his light heaven and earth would have been invisible and undistinguishable. The next poet says that Agni held heaven aloft by his light, that he kept the two world as under; and in the end Agni is said to be the progenitor and father of heaven and earth, and in the maker of all that flies, or walks, or stands, or moves on earth.

Here we have once more the same process before our eyes. The human mind begins with being startled by a single or repeated event, such as the lightning striking a tree and devouring a whole forest, or a spark of fire breaking forth from wood being rubbed against wood, whether in a forest, or in the wheel of a carriage, or at last in a fire-drill, devised on purpose. Man then begins to wonder at what to him is a miracle, none the less so because it is a fact, a simple, natural fact. He sees the effects of a power, but he can only guess at its cause, and if he is to speak of it, he can only do so by speaking of it as an agent, or as something like a human agent, and, if in some respects not quite human, in others more than human or super-human. Thus the concept of fire grew, and while it became more and more generalised, it also became more sublime, more incomprehensible, more divine. Without Agni, without fire, light, and warmth, life would have been impossible. Hence he became the author and giver of life, of the life of plants and animals and of men; and his favour having once been implored for 'light and life and all things,' what wonder that in the minds of some poets, and in the traditions of this or that village community, he should have been raised to the rank of a supreme ruler, a god above all gods, their own true god!

We now proceed to consider the powers which the ancient poets might have discovered in the air, in the clouds, and, more particularly, in those meteoric conflicts which by thunder, lightning, darkness, storms, and showers of rain must have taught man that very important lesson that he was not alone in this world. Many philosophers, as you know, believe that all religion arose from fear or terror, and that without thunder and lightning to teach us, we should never have believed in any gods or god. This is a one-sided and exaggerated view. Thunderstorms, no doubt, had a large share in arousing feelings of awe and terror, and in making man conscious of his weakness and dependence. Even in the Veda Indra is introduced as saying: 'Yes, when I send thunder and lightning, then you believe in me.' But what we call religion would never have sprung from fear and terror alone. *Religion is trust*, and that trust arose in the beginning from the impressions made on the mind and heart of man by the order and wisdom of nature, and more particularly, by those regularly recurring events, the return of the sun, the revival of the moon, the order of the seasons, the law of cause and effect, gradually discovered in all things, and traced back in the end to a cause of all causes, by whatever name we choose to call it.

Still, the meteoric phenomena had, no doubt, their important share in the production of ancient deities; and in the poems of the Vedic *rishis* they naturally occupy a very prominent place. If we were asked who was the principal god of the Vedic period, we should probably, judging from the remains of that poetry which we possess, say it was Indra, the god of the blue sky, the Indian Zeus, the gatherer of the clouds, the giver of rain, the wielder of the thunderbolt, the conqueror of darkness and of all the powers of darkness, the bringer of light, the source of freshness, vigour, and life, the ruler and lord of the whole world. Indra is this, and much more in the Veda. He is supreme in the hymns of many poets, and may have been so in the prayers-addressed to him by many of the ancient septs or village communities in India. Compared with him the other gods are said to be decrepit old men. Heaven, the old heaven or Dyaus, formerly the father of all the gods, nay the father of Indra himself, bows before him, and the Earth trembles at his approach. Yet Indra never commanded the permanent allegiance of all the other gods like Zeus and Jupiter; nay, we know from the Veda itself that there were sceptics, even at that early time, who denied that there was any such thing as Indra.

By the side of Indra, and associated with him in his battles, and sometimes hardly distinguishable from him, we find the representatives of the wind, called Vata or Vayu, and the more terrible Storm-gods, the Maruts, literally the Smashers.

When speaking of the Wind, a poet says: 'Where was he born? Whence did he spring? the life of the gods, the germ of the world!

That god moves about where he listeth, his voices are heard, but he is not to be seen.'

The Maruts are more terrible than Vata, the wind. They are clearly the representatives of such storms as are known in India, when the air is darkened by dust and clouds, when in a moment the trees are stripped of their foliage, their branches shivered, their stems snapped, when the earth seems to reel and the mountains to shake, and the rivers are lashed into foam and fury. Then the poet sees the Maruts approaching with golden helmets, with spotted skins on their shoulders, brandishing golden spears, whirling their axes, shooting fiery arrows, and cracking their whips amidst thunder and lightning. They are the comrades of Indra, sometimes, like Indra, the sons of Dyaus or the sky, but also the sons of another terrible god, called Rudra, or the Howler, a fighting god, to whom many hymns are addressed. In him a new character is evolved, that of a healer and saviour,— a very natural transition in India, where nothing is so powerful for dispelling *miasmas*, restoring health, and imparting fresh vigour to man and beast, as a thunderstorm, following after weeks of heat and drought.

All these and several others, such as Parjanya and the Ribhus, are the gods of mid-air, the most active and dramatic gods, ever present to the fancy of the ancient poets, and in several cases, the prototypes of later heroes, celebrated in the epic poems of India. In battles, more particularly, these fighting gods of the sky were constantly invoked. Indra is the leader in battles, the protector of the bright Aryans, the destroyer of the black aboriginal inhabitants of India. 'He has thrown down fifty thousand black fellows,' the poet says, 'and their strongholds crumbled away like an old rag.' Strange to say, Indra is praised for having saved his people from their enemies, much as Jehovah was praised by the Jewish prophets. Thus we read in one hymn that when Sudas, the pious king of the Tritsus, was pressed hard in his battle with the ten kinds, Indra changed the flood into an easy ford, and thus saved Sudas.

In another hymn we read: 'Thou hast restrained the great river for the sake of Turviti Vayya: the flood moved in obedience to thee, and thou madest the rivers easy to corss.' This is not very different from the *Psalmist* (LXXVIII.13): 'He divided the sea, and caused them to pass through; and he made the waters to stand as an heap.'

And there are other passages which have reminded some students of the Veda of Joshua's battle, when the sun stood still and the moon stayed, until the people had avenged themselves upon their enemies. For we read in the Veda also that 'Indra lengthened the days into the night,' and that 'the Sun unharnessed his chariot in the middle of the day.'

In some of the hymns addressed to Indra his original connection with the sky and the thunderstorm seems quite forgotten. He has become a spiritual god, the only king of all worlds and all people, who sees and hears everything, nay, who inspires men with their best thoughts. No one is equal to him, no one excels him.

The name of Indra is peculiar to India, and must have been formed after the separation of the great Aryan family had taken place, for we find it neither in Greek, nor in Latin, nor in German. There are Vedic gods, as I mentioned before, whose names must have been framed before that separation, and which occur therefore, though greatly modified in character, sometimes in Greek, sometimes in Latin, sometimes in the Celtic, Teutonic, and Slavonic dialects. Dyaus, for instance, is the same word as Zeus or Jupiter, Ushas is Eos, Nakta is Nyx, Surya is Helios, Agni is ignis, Bhaga is Baga in Old Persian, Bogu in Old Slavonic, Varuna is Uranos, Vak is vox. and in the name of the *Maruts*, or the storm-gods, the germs of the Italic god of war, Mars, have been discovered. Besides these direct coincidences, some indirect relations have been established between Hermes and Sarameya, Dionysos and Dyunisya, Prometheus and Pramantha, Orpheus and Ribhu, Erinnys and Saranyu, Pan and Pavana.

But while the name of Indra as the god of the sky, also as the god of the thunderstorm, and the giver of rain, is unknown among the North-western members of the Aryan family, the name of another god who sometimes acts the part of Indra, but is much less prominent in the Veda, I mean Parjanya, must have existed before that of Indra, because two at least of the Aryan languages have carried it, as we shall see, to Germany, and to the very shores of the Baltic.

Sometimes this Parjanya stands in the place of Dyaus, the sky. Thus we read in the *Atharvaveda*: 'The Earth is the mother, and I am the son of the Earth. Parjanya is the father; may he help us!'

In another place the earth, instead of being the wife of heaven or Dyaus, is called the wife of Parjanya.

Now who or what is this Parjanya? There have been long controversies about him, as to whether he is the same as Dyaus, heaven, or the same as Indra, the successor of Dyaus, whether he is the god of the sky, of the cloud, or of the rain.

To me it seems that this very expression, god of the sky, god of the cloud, is so entire an anachronism that we could not even translate it into Vedic Sanskrit without committing a solecism. It is true, no doubt, we must use our modern ways of speaking when we wish to represent the thoughts of the ancient world; but we cannot be too much on our guard against accepting the dictionary representative of an ancient word for its real counterpart. Deva, no doubt, means 'gods' and 'god', and Parjanya means 'cloud', but no one could say in Sanskrit *parjanyasya devah*, 'the god of the cloud.' The god, or the divine or transcendental element, does not come from without, to be added to the cloud or to the sky or to the earth, but it springs from the cloud and the sky and the earth, and is slowly elaborated into an independent concept. As many words in ancient languages have an undefined meaning, and lend themselves to various purposes according to the various intentions of the speakers, the names of the gods also share in this elastic and plastic character of ancient speech. There are passages where Parjanya means cloud, there are passages where it means rain. There are passages where Parjanya takes the place which elsewhere is filled by Dyaus, the sky, or by Indra, the active god of the atmosphere. This may seem very wrong and very unscientific to the scientific mythologist. But it cannot be helped. It is the nature of ancient thought and ancient language to be unscientific, and we must learn to master it as well as we can, instead of finding fault with it, and complaining that our forefathers did not reason exactly as we do.

There are passages in the Vedic hymns where Parjanya appears as a supreme god. He is called father, like Dyaus, the sky. He is called *asura*, the living or life-giving god, a name peculiar to the oldest and the greatest gods. One poet says, 'He rules as god over the whole world; all creatures rest in him; he is the life (*atma*) of all that moves and rests.'

Surely it is difficult to say more of a supreme god than what is here said of Parjanya. Yet in other hymns he is represented as performing his office, namely that of sending rain upon the earth, under the control of Mitra and Varuna, who are then considered as the highest lords, the mightiest rulers of heaven and earth.

There are other verses, again, where Parjanya occurs with hardly any traces of personality, but simply as a name of cloud or rain.

Thus we read: 'Even by day the Maruts (the storm gods) produce darkness with the cloud that carries water, when they moisten the earth.' Here cloud is Parjanya, and it is evidently used as an appellative, and not as a proper name. The same word occurs in the plural also, and we read of many Parjanyas or clouds vivifying the earth.

When Devapi prays for rain in favour of his brother, he says: 'O lord of my prayer (Brihaspati), whether thou be Mitra or Varuna or Pushan, come to my sacrifice! Whether thou be together with the Adityas, the Vasus or the Maruts, let the cloud (Parjanya) rain for Santanu.'

And again: 'Stir up the rainy cloud' (Parjanya)

In several places it makes no difference whether we translate Parjanya by cloud or by rain, for those who pray for rain, pray for the cloud, and whatever may be the benefits of the rain, they may nearly all be called the benefits of the cloud. There is a curious hymn, for instance, addressed to the frogs who, at the beginning of the rains, come forth from the dry ponds, and embrace each other and chatter together, and whom the poet compares to priests singing at a sacrifice, a not very complimentary remarks from a poet who is himself supposed to have been a priest. Their voice is said to have been revived by Parjanya, which we shall naturally translate by rain, though, no doubt, the poet may have meant, for all we know, either a cloud, or even the god Parjanya himself.

I shall try to translate one of the hymns addressed to Parjanya, when conceived as a god, or at least as so much of the god as it was possible to be at that stage in the intellectual growth of the human race.

1. 'Invoke the strong god with these songs! praise Parjanya, worship him with veneration! for he, the roaring bull, scattering drops, gives seed-fruit to plants.

2. 'He cuts the trees asunder, he kills evil spirits; the whole world trembles before his mighty weapon. Even the guiltless flees before the powerful, when Parjanya thundering strikes down the evil-doers.

3. 'Like a charioteer, striking his horses with a whip, he puts forth his messengers of rain. From afar arise the roarings of the lion, when Parjanya makes the sky full of rain.

4. 'The winds blow, the lightnings fly, plants spring up, the sky pours. Food is produced for the whole world, when Parjanya blesses the earth with his seed.

5. 'O Parjanya, thou at whose work the earth bows down, thou at whose work hoofed animals are scattered, thou at whose work the plants assume all forms, grant thou to us thy great protection!

6. 'O Maruts, give us the rain of heaven, make the streams of the strong horse run down! And come thou hither with thy thunder, pouring out water, for thou (O Parjanya) art the living god, thou art our father.

7. 'Do thou roar, and thunder, and give fruitfulness! Fly around us with thy chariot full of water! Draw forth thy water-skin, when it has been opened and turned downward, and let the high and the low places become level!

8. 'Draw up the large bucket, and pour it out; let the streams pour forth freely! Soak heaven and earth with fatness! and let there be a good draught for the cows!

9. 'O Parjanya, when roaring and thundering thou killest the evil-doers, then everything rejoices, whatever lives on earth.

10. 'Thou hast sent rain, stop now! Thou hast made the deserts passable, thou hast made plants grow for food, and thou hast obtained praise from men.'

This is a Vedic hymn, and a very fair specimen of what these ancient hymns are. There is nothing very grand and poetical about them, and yet, I say, take thousands and thousands of people living in our villages and depending on rain for their very life, and not many of them will be able to compose such a prayer for rain, even though three thousand years have passed over our heads since Parjanya was first invoked in India. Nor are these verses entirely without poetical conceptions and descriptions. Whoever has watched a real thunder-storm in a hot climate, will recognise the truth of those quick sentences, 'the winds blow, the lightnings fly, plants spring up, the hoofed cattle are scattered.' Nor is the idea without a certain drastic reality, that Parjanya draws a bucket of water from his well in heaven, and pours out skin after skin (in which water was then carried) down upon the earth.

There is even a moral sentiment perceptible in this hymn. 'When the storms roar and the lightnings flash and the rain pours down, even the guiltless trembles, and evildoers are struck down.' Here we clearly see that the poet did not look upon the storm simply as an outbreak of the violence of nature, but that he had a presentiment of a higher will and power which even the guiltless fears; for who, he seems to say, is entirely free from guilt?

If now we ask again, Who is Parjanya? or What is Parjanya? we can answer that Parjanya was meant originally for the cloud, so far as it gives rain; but as soon as the idea of a giver arose, the visible cloud became the outward appearance only, or the body of that giver, and the giver himself was somewhere else, we know not where. In some verses Parjanya seems to step into the place of Dyaus, the sky, and Prithivi, the earth, is his wife. In other places, however, he is the son of Dyaus or the sky, though no thought is given in that early stage to the fact that thus Parjanya might seem to be the husband of his mother. We saw that even the idea of Indra being the father of his own father did not startle the ancient poets beyond an exclamation that it was a very wonderful thing indeed.

Sometimes Parjanya does the work of Indra, the Jupiter Pluvius of the Veda; sometimes of Vayu, the wind, sometimes of Soma, the giver of rain. Yet with all this he is not Dyaus, nor Indra, nor the Maruts, nor Vayu, nor Soma. He stands by himself, a separate person, a separate god, as we should say— nay, one of the oldest of all the Aryan gods.

If derived from *parj,* to sprinkle, Parjanya would have meant originally 'he who irrigates or gives rain.'

When the different members of the Aryan family dispersed, they might all of them, the ancestors of Hindus as well as of Greeks and Celts, and Teutons and Slays, have carried that name for cloud with them. But you know that it happened very often that out of the common wealth of their ancient language,one and the same word was preserved as the case might be, not by all, but by only six, or five, or four, or three, or two, or even by one only of the seven principal heirs; and yet, as we know that there was no historical contact between them, after they had once parted from each other, long before the beginning of what we call history, the fact that two of the Aryan languages have preserved the same finished word with the same finished meaning, is proof sufficient that it belonged to the most ancient treasure of Aryan thought.

Now there is no trace, at least no very clear trace, of Parjanya, in Greek or Latin or Celtic, or even in Teutonic. In Slavonic, too, we look in vain, till we come to that almost forgotten side-branch called the Lettic, comprising the spoken Lituanian and Lettish, and the now extinct Old Prussian. The Lituanian language, even as it is now spoken by the common people, contains some extremely primitive grammatical forms—in some cases almost identical with Sanskrit. These forms are all the more curious, because they are but few in number, and the rest of the language has suffered much from the wear and tear of centuries.

Now in that remote Lituanian language we find that our old friend Parjanya has taken refuge. There he lives to the present day, while even in India he is almost forgotten, at least in the spoken languages; and there, in Lituania, not many centuries back might be heard among a Christianised or nearly Christianised people, prayers for rain, not very different from that which I translated to you from the *Rigveda*. In Lituanian the god of thunder was called Perkunas, and the same word is still used in the sense of thunder. In Old Prussian, thunder was *percunos*, and in Lettish to the present day *perkons* is thunder, god of thunder.

It was, I believe, Grimm who for the first time identified the Vedic Parjanya with the Old Slavonic Perun, the Polish Piorun, the Bohemian Peraun. These words had formerly been derived by Dobrowsky and others from the root *peru*, I strike. Grimm showed that the fuller forms Perkunas, Pehrkons, and Perkunos existed in Lituanian, Lettish, Old Prussian, and that even the Mordvinians had adopted the name Porguini as that of their thunder-god.

Among the neighbours of the Lets, the Esthomans, who, though un-Aryan in language, have evidently learnt much from their Aryan neighbours, the following prayer was heard, addressed by an old peasant to their god Picker or Picken, the god of thunder and rain, as late as the seventeenth century:

'Dear Thunder (woda Picker) we offer to thee an ox that has two horns and four cloven hoofs; we would pray thee for our ploughing and sowing; that our straw be copper-red, our grain golden-yellow. Push elsewhere all the thick black clouds, over great fens, high forests, and wildernesses. But unto us, ploughers and sowers, give a fruitful season and sweet rain. Holy Thunder (poha Picken), guard our seed-field, that it bear good straw below, good ears above, and good grain within.'

Now, I say again, I do not wish you to admire this primitive poetry, primitive, whether it is repeated in the Esthonian fens in the seventeenth century of our era, or sung in the valley of the Indus in the seventeenth century before our era. Let aesthetic critics say what they like about these uncouth poems. I only ask you, is it not worth a great many poems, to have established this fact, that the same god Parjanya, the god of clouds and thunder and lightning and rain, who was invoked in India a thousand years before India was discovered by Alexander, should have been remembered and believed in by Lituanian peasants on the frontier between East Prussia and Russia, not more than two hundred years ago, and should have retained its old name Parjanya, which in Sanskrit meant 'showering,' under the form of Perkuna, which in Lituanian is a name and a name only, wihout any etymological meaning at all; nay, should live on, as some scholars assure us, in an abbreviated form in most Slavonic dialects, namely, in Old Slavonic as Perun, in Polish as Piorun, in Bohemian as Peraun, all meaning thunder or thunder-storm?

Such facts strike me as if we saw the blood suddenly beginning to flow again through the veins of old mummies; or as if the Egyptian statues of black granite were suddenly to begin to speak to us. Touched by the rays of modern science the old words —call them mummies or statues—begin indeed to live again, the old names of gods and heroes begin indeed to speak again. All that is old becomes new, all that is new becomes old, and that one word, Parjanya, seems, like a charm, to open before our eyes the cave or cottage in which the fathers of the Aryan race, our own fathers,—whether we live on the Baltic or on the Indian Ocean,—are seen gathered together, taking refuge from the buckets of Parjanya, and saying: 'Stop now, Parjanya; thou hast sent rain; thou hast made the deserts passable, and hast made the plants to grow; and thou hast obtained praise from man.'

We have still to consider the third class of gods, in addition to the gods of the earth and the sky, namely the gods of the highest heaven, more serene in their character than the active and fighting gods of the air and the clouds, and more remote from the eyes of man, and therefore more mysterious in the exercise of their power than the gods of the earth or the air.

The principal deity is here no doubt the bright sky itself, the old Dyaus, worshipped as we know by the Aryas before they broke up into separate people and languages, and surviving in Greece as Zeus, in Italy as Jupiter, Heaven-father, and among the Teutonic tribes as *Tyr* and *Tiu*. In the Veda we saw him chiefly invoked in connection with the earth, as Dyavaprithivi, Heaven and Earth. He is invoked by himself also, but he is a vanishing god, and his place is taken in most of the Vedic poems by the younger and more active god, *Indra*.

Another representative of the highest heaven, as covering, embracing, and shielding all things, is Varuna, a name derived from the root var, to cover, and identical with the Greek Ouranos. This god is one of the most interesting creations of the Hindu mind, because though we can still perceive the physical background from which he rises, the vast, starry, brilliant expanse above, his features, more than those of any of the Vedic gods, have become completely transfigured, and he stands before us as a god who watches over the world, punishes the evil-doer, and even forgives the sins of those who implore his pardon.

I shall read you one of the hymns addressed to him:

'Let us be blessed in thy service, O Varuna, for we always think of thee and praise thee, greeting thee day by day, like the fires lighted on the altar, at the approach of the rich dawns.' 2.

'O Varuna , our guide, let us stand in thy keeping, thou who art rich in heroes and praised far and wide! And you, unconquered sons of Aditi, deign to accept us as your friends. O gods!' 3.

'Aditya, the ruler, sent forth these rivers; they follow the law of Varuna. They tire not, they cease not; like birds they fly quickly everywhere.' 4.

'Take from me my sin, like a fetter, and we shall increase, O Varuna, the spring of thy law. Let not the thread be cut while I weave my song! Let not the form of the workman break before the time!'5.

'Take far away from me this terror, O Varuna! Thou, O righteous king, have mercy on me! Like as a rope from a calf, remove from me my sin; for away from thee I am not master even of the twinkling of an eye.' 6.

'Do not strike us, Varuna, with weapons which at thy will hurt the evil-doer. Let us not go where the light has vanished ! Scatter our enemies, that we may live.' 7.

'We did formerly, O Varuna, and do now, and shall in future also, sing praises to thee, O mighty one! For on thee, unconquerable hero, rest all statutes, immovable, as if established on a rock.' 8.

'Move far away from me all self-committed guilt, and may I not, O king, suffer for what others have committed! Many dawns have not yet dawned; grant us to live in them, O Varuna.' 9.

You may have observed that in this hymn Varuna was called Aditya, or son of Aditi. Now Aditi means *infinitude,* from *dita,* bound, and *a,* not, that is, not bound, not limited, absolute, infinite. Aditi itself is now and then invoked in the Veda, as the Beyond, as what is beyond the earth and the sky, and the sun and the dawn—a most surprising conception in that early period of religious thought. More frequently, however, than Aditi, we meet with the Adityas, literally the sons of Aditi, or the gods beyond the visible earth and sky,— in one sense, the infinite gods. One of them is Varuna, others Mitra and Aryaman (Bhaga, Daksha, Amsa), most of them abstract names, though pointing to heaven and the solar light of heaven as their first, though almost forgotten source.

When Mitra and Varuna are invoked together, we can still perceive dimly that they were meant originally for day and night, light and darkness. But in their more personal and so to say dramatic aspect, day and night appear in the Vedic mythology as the two Asvins, the two horsemen.

Aditi, too, the infinite, still shows a few traces of her being originally connected with the boundless dawn; but again, in her more personal and dramatic character, the dawn is praised by the Vedic poets as Ushas, the Greek Eos, the beautiful maid of the morning, loved by the Asvins, loved by the sun, but vanishing before him at the very moment when he tries to embrace her with his golden rays. The sun himself, whom we saw reflected several times before in some of the divine personifications of the air and the sky and even of the earth, appears once more in his full personality, as the sun of the sky, under the names of Surya (Helios), Savitri, Pushan, and Vishnu, and many more.

You see from all this how great a mistake it would be to attempt to reduce the whole of Aryan mythology to solar concepts, and to solar concepts only. We have seen how largely the earth, the air, and the sky have each contributed their share to the earliest religious and mythological treasury of the Vedic Aryas. Nevertheless, the sun occupied in that ancient collection of Aryan thought, which we call Mythology, the same central and commanding position which, under different names, it still holds in our own thoughts.

What we call the Morning, the ancient Aryas called the Sun or the Dawn; 'and there is no solemnity so deep to a rightly thinking creature as that of the Dawn.' (These are not my words, but the words of one of our greatest poets, one of the truest worshippers of Nature—John Ruskin). What we call Noon, and Evening, and Night, what we call Spring and Winter, what we call Year, and Time, and Life, and Eternity—all this the ancient Aryas called Sun. And yet wise people wonder and say, how curious that the ancient Aryas should have had so many solar myths. Why, every time we say 'Good Morning', we commit a solar myth. Every poet who sings about 'the May driving the Winter from the field again' commits a solar myth. Every 'Christmas Number' of our newspapers— ringing out the old year and ringing in the new— is brimful of solar myths. Be not afraid of solar myths, but whenever in ancient mythology you meet with a name that, according to the strictest phonetic rules (for this is a *sine qua non*), can be traced back to a word meaning sun, or dawn, or morning, or night, or spring or winter, accept it for what it was meant to be, and do not be greatly surprised, if a story told of a solar eponymos was originally a solar myth.

No one has more strongly protested against the extravagances of Comparative Mythologists in changing everything into solar legends, than I have; but if I read some of the arguments brought forward against this new science, I confess they remind me of nothing so much as of the arguments brought forward, centuries ago, against the existence of Antipodes! People then appealed to what is called Common Sense, which ought to teach everybody that Antipodes could not possibly exist, because they would tumble off. The best answer that astronomers could give, was, 'Go and see.' And I can give no better answer to those learned sceptics who try to ridicule the Science of Comparative Mythology— 'Go and see!' that is, go and read the Veda, and before you have finished the first Mandala, I can promise you, you will no longer shake your wise heads at solar myths, whether in India, or in Greece, or in Italy, or even in England, where we see so little of the sun, and talk all the more about the weather— that is, about a solar myth.

We have thus seen from the hymns and prayers preserved to us in the *Rigveda*, how a large number of so-called Devas, bright and sunny beings, or gods, were called into existence, how the whole world was peopled with them, and every act of nature, whether on the earth or in the air or in the highest heaven, ascribed to their agency. When we say, *it* thunders, they said Indra thunders; when we say, *it* rains, they said Parjanya pours out his buckets; when we say, *it* dawns, they said the beautiful Ushas appears like a dancer, displaying her splendour; when we say, *it* grows dark, they said Surya unharnesses his steeds. The whole of nature was alive to the poets of the Veda, the presence of the gods was felt everywhere, and in that sentiment of the presence of the gods there was a germ of religious morality, sufficiently strong, it would seem, to restrain people from committing as it were before the eyes of their gods what they were ashamed to commit before the eyes of men. When speaking of Varuna, the old god of the sky, one poet says:

'Varuna, the great lord of these worlds, sees as if he were near. If a man stands or walks or hides, if he goes to lie down or to get up, what two people sitting together whisper to each other, King Varuna knows it, he is there as the third. This earth, too, belongs to Varuna, the King, and this wide sky with its ends far apart. The two seas (the sky and the ocean) are Varuna's loins; he is also contained in this small drop of water. He who should flee far beyond the sky, even he would not be rid of Varuna, the King. His spies proceed from heaven towards this world; with thousand eyes they overlook this earth. King Varuna sees all this, what is between heaven and earth, and what is beyond. He has counted the twinklings of the eyes of men. As a player throws down the dice, he settles all things (irrevocably). May all thy fatal snares which stand spread out seven by seven and threefold, catch the man who tells a lie, may they pass by him who speaks the truth.'

You see this is as beautiful, and in some respects as true, as anything in the *Psalms.* And yet we know that there never was such a Deva, or god, or such a thing as Varuna. We know it is a mere name, meaning originally 'covering or all-embracing,' which was applied to the visible starry sky, and afterwards, by a process perfectly intelligible, developed into the name of a Being behind the starry sky, endowed with human and superhuman qualities.

And what applies to Varuna applies to all the other gods of the Veda and the Vedic religion, whether three in number, or thirty-three, or, as one poet said, 'three thousand three hundred and thirty-nine gods.' They are all but names, quite as much as Jupiter and Apollo and Minerva; in fact, quite as much as all the gods of every religion who are called by such appellative titles.

Possibly, if any one had said this during the Vedic age in India, or even during the Periclean age in Greece, he would have been called, like Socrates, a blasphemer or an atheist. And yet nothing can be clearer or truer, and we shall see that some of the poets of the Veda too, and, still more, the later Vedantic philosopher, had a clear insight that it was so.

Only let us be careful in the use of that phrase 'it is a mere name.' No name is a mere name. Every name was originally meant for something; only it often failed to express what it was meant to express, and then became a weak or an empty name, or what we then call 'a mere name.' So it was with these names of the Vedic gods. They were all meant to express the *Beyond,* the Invisible behind the Visible, the Infinite within the Finite, the Supernatural above the Natural, the Divine, omnipresent, and omnipotent. They failed in expressing what, by its very nature, must always remain inexpressible. But that Inexpressible itself remained, and in spite of all these failures, it never succumbed, or vanished from the mind of the ancient thinkers and poets, but always called for new and better names, nay calls for them even now, and will call for them to the very end of the man's existence upon earth.

Notes

Pages

111. Phlegyas: Legendary king of the Lapithes, a mythical people of Thessaly. Kuhn (Adalbert) German linguist (1812-81), well known as an authority on Indo-European languages.
114. Joshua's battle: *Old Testament*, Joshua, X, 13.
117. Devapi: obtained rain for the kingdom of his younger brother after a drought of twelve years. The drought was attributed to the younger brother having superseded the elder.
120. Mordvinians: A Finnish people of Eastern Russia.
125. Periclean age: The most brilliant period of Greek history, fifth century BC. Pericles, orator and statesman, was the greatest figure in Athens, then the most powerful city in Greece.

LECTURE VII

Veda and Vedanta

I DO NOT wonder that I should have been asked by some of my hearers to devote part of my last lecture to answering the question, how the Vedic literature could have been composed and preserved, if writing was unknown in India before 500 BC, while the hymns of the *Rigveda* are said to date from 1500 BC. Classical scholars naturally ask what is the date of our oldest MSS of the *Rigveda*, and what is the evidence on which so high an antiquity is assigned to its contents? I shall try to answer this question as well as I can, and I shall begin with a humble confession that the oldest MSS of the *Rigveda*, known to us at present, date not from 1500 BC but from about AD 1500.

We have therefore a gap of three thousand years, which it will require a strong arch of argument to bridge over.

But that is not all.

You may know how, in the beginning of this century, when the age of the Homeric poems was discussed, a German scholar, Frederick August Wolf, asked two momentous questions:

1. At what time did the Greeks first become acquainted with the alphabet and use it for inscriptions on public monuments, coins, shields, and for contracts, both public and private?

2. At what time did the Greeks first think of using writing for literary purposes, and what materials did they employ for that purpose?

These two questions and the answer they elicited threw quite a new light on the nebulous periods of Greek literature. A fact more firmly established than any other in the ancient history of Greece is that the Ionians learnt the alphabet from the Phoenicians. The Ionians always called their letters Phoenician letters, and the very name of Alphabet was a Phoenician word. We can well understand that the Phoenicians should have taught the Ionians in Asia Minor a knowledge of the alphabet, partly for commercial purposes, i.e. for making contracts, partly for enabling them to use those useful little sheets, called *Periplus*, or *Circumnavigations*, which at that time were as precious to sailors as maps were to the adventurous seamen of the middle ages. But from that to a written literature, in our sense of the word, there is still a wide step. It is well known that the Germans, particularly in the North, had their Runes for inscriptions on tombs, goblets, public monuments, but not for literary purposes. Even if a few Ionians at Miletus and other centres of political and commercial life acquired the art of writing, where could they find writing materials? and, still more important, where could they find readers? The Ionians, when they began to write, had to be satisfied with a hide or pieces of leather, which they called *diphthera* and until that was brought to the perfection of vellum or parchment, the occupation of an author cannot have been very agreeable.

So far as we know at present the Ionians began to write about the middle of the sixth century BC; and, whatever may have been said to the contrary, Wolf's *dictum* still holds good that with them the beginning of a written literature was the same as the beginning of prose writing.

Writing at that time was an effort, and such an effort was made for some great purpose only. Hence the first written skins were what we should call Murray's Handbooks, called *Periegesis* or *Periodos*, or, if treating of sea-voyages, *Periplus*, that is, guidebooks, books to lead travellers round a country or round a town. Connected with these itineraries were the accounts of the foundations of cities, the *Ktisis*. Such books existed in Asia Minor during the sixth and fifth centuries, and their writers were called by a general term, *logographi*, or *logioi* or *logopoioi*, as opposed to *aoidoi*, the poets. They were the forerunners of the Greek historians, and Herodotus (443 BC), the so-called father of history, made frequent use of their works.

The whole of this incipient literary activity belonged to Asia Minor. From 'Guides through towns and countries,' literature seems to have spread at an early time to Guides through life, or philosophical dicta, such as are ascribed to Anaximander the Ionian (610-547 BC), and Pherekydes the Syrian (540 BC). These names carry us into the broad daylight of history, for Anaximander was the teacher of Anaximences, Anaximenes of Anaxagoras, and Anaxagoras of Pericles. At that time writing was a recognised art, and its cultivation had been rendered possible chiefly through trade with Egypt and the importation of *papyros.* In the time of Æschylos (500 BC) the idea of writing had become so familiar that he could use it again and again in poetical metaphors, and there seems little reason why we should doubt that both Peisistratos (528 BC) and Polykrates of Samos (523 BC) were among the first collectors of Greek manuscripts.

In this manner the simple questions asked by Wolf helped to reduce the history of ancient Greek literature to some kind of order, particularly with reference to its first beginnings.

It would therefore seem but reasonable that the two first questions to be asked by the students of Sanskrit literature should have been:

1. At what time did the people of India become acquainted with an alphabet?

2. At what time did, they first use such alphabet for literary purposes?

Curiously enough, however, these questions remained in abeyance for a long time, and, as a consequence, it was impossible to introduce even the first elements of order into the chaos of ancient Sanskrit literature.

I can here state a few facts only. There are no inscriptions to be found anywhere in India before the middle of the third century BC. These inscriptions are Buddhist, put up during the reign of Asoka, the grandson of Chandragupta, who was the contemporary of Seleucus, and at whose court in Pataliputra Megasthenes lived as ambassador of Seleucus. Here, as you see, we are on historical ground. In fact, there is little doubt that Asoka, the king who put up these inscriptions in several parts of his vast kingdom, reigned from 274-237 BC.

These inscriptions are written in two alphabets—one written from right to left, and clearly derived from an Aramæan, that is, a Semitic alphabet; the other written from left to right, and likewise an adaptation, and an artificial or systematic adaptation, of a Semitic alphabet to the requirements of of an Indian language. That second alphabet became the source of all Indian alphabets, and of many alphabets carried chiefly by Buddhist teachers far beyond the limits of India, though it is possible that the earliest Tamil alphabet may have been directly derived from the same Semitic source which supplied with the *dextrorsum* and the *sinistrorsum* alphabets of India.

Here then we have the first fact, viz., that writing, even for monumental purposes, was unknown in India before the third century BC.

But writing for commercial purposes was known in India before that time. Megasthenes was no doubt quite right when he said that the Indians did not know letters, that their laws were not written, and that they administered justice from memory. But Nearchus, the admiral of Alexander the Great, who sailed down the Indus (325 BC), and was therefore brought in contact with the merchants frequenting the maritime stations of India, was probably equally right in declaring that 'the Indians wrote letters on cotton that had been well beaten together.' These were no doubt commercial documents, contracts, it may be, with Phoenician or Egyptian captains, and they would prove nothing as to the existence in India at that time of what we mean by a written literature. In fact, Nearchus himself affirms what Megasthenes said after him, namely that 'the laws of the sophists in India were not written.' If, at the same time, the Greek travellers in India speak of mile-stones, and of cattle marked by the Indians with various signs and also with numbers, all this would perfectly agree with what we know from other sources, that though the art of writing may have reached India before the time of Alexander's conquest, its employment for literary purposes cannot date from a much earlier time.

Here then we are brought face to face with a most startling fact. Writing was unknown in India before the fourth century before Christ, and yet we are asked to believe that the Vedic literature in its three well-defined periods, the Mantra, Brahmana, and Sutra periods, goes back to at least a thousand years before our era.

Now the *Rigveda* alone, which contains a collection of ten books of hymns addressed to various deities, consists of 1017 (1028) poems, 10,580 verses, and about 153,826 words. How were these poems composed—for they are composed in very perfect metre—and how, after having being composed, were they handed down from 1500 before Christ to 1500 after Christ, the time to which most of our best Sanskrit MSS belong?

Entirely by memory: This may sound startling, but—what will sound still more startling, and yet is a fact that can easily be ascertained by anybody who doubts it—at the present moment, if every MS of the *Rigveda* were lost, we should be able to recover the whole of it—from the memory of the Srotriyas in India. These native students learn the Veda by heart, and they learn it from the mouth of their *guru*, never from a MS, still less from my printed edition,—and after a time they teach it again to their pupils.

I have had such students in my room at Oxford, who not only could repeat these hymns, but who repeated them with the proper accents (for the Vedic Sanskrit has accents like Greek), nay who, when looking through my printed edition of the *Rigveda*, could point out a misprint without the slightest hesitation.

I can tell you more. There are hardly any various readings in our MSS of the *Rigveda*, but various schools in India have their own readings of certain passages, and they hand down those readings with great care. So, instead of collating MSS as we do in Greek and Latin, I have asked some friends of mine to collate those Vedic students, who carry their own *Rigveda* in their memory, and to let me have the various readings from these living authorities.

Here then we are not dealing with theories, but with facts, which anybody may verify. The whole of the *Rigveda*, and a great deal more, still exists at the present moment in the oral tradition of a number of scholars who, if they liked, could write down every letter, and every accent, exactly as we find them in our old MSS.

Of course, this learning by heart is carried on under a strict discipline; it is, in fact, considered as a sacred duty. A native friend of mine, himself a very distinguished Vedic scholar, tells me that a boy, who is to be brought up as a student of the *Rigveda*, has to spend about eight years in the house of his teacher. He has to learn ten books: first, the hymns of the *Rigveda*; then a prose treatise on sacrifices, called the Brahmana; then the so-called Forest-book or Aranyaka; then the rules on domestic ceremonies; and lastly, six treatises on pronunciation, grammar, etymology, metre, astronomy, and ceremonial.

These ten books it has been calculated contain nearly 30,000 lines, each line reckoned as thirty-two syllables.

A pupil studies every day, during the eight years of his theological apprenticeship, except on the holidays, which are called 'non-reading days.' There being 360 days in a lunar year, the eight years would give him 2,880 days. Deduct from this 384 holidays, and you get 2,496 working days during the eight years. If you divide the number of lines, 30,000, by the number of working days, you get about twelve lines to be learnt each day, though much time is taken up, in addition, for practising and rehearsing what has been learnt before.

Now this is the state of things at present, though I doubt whether it will last much longer, and I always impress on my friends in India, and therefore impress on those also who will soon be settled as Civil Servants in India, the duty of trying to learn all that can still be learnt from those living libraries. Much ancient Sanskrit lore will be lost for ever when that race of Srotriyas becomes extinct.

But now let us look back. About a thousand years ago a Chinese, of the name of I-tsing, a Buddhist, went to India to learn Sanskrit, in order to be able to translate some of the sacred books of his own religion, which were originally written in Sanskrit, into Chinese. He left China in 671, twenty-five years after Hiuen-tsang's return, arrived at Tamralipti in India in 673, and went to the great College and Monastery of Nalanda, where he studied Sanskrit. He returned to China in 695, and died in 713.

In one of his works which we still possess in Chinese, he gives an account of what he saw in India, not only among his own co-religionists, the Buddhists, but likewise among the Brahmans.

Of the Buddhist priests he says that after they have learnt to recite the five and the ten precepts, they are taught the 400 hymns of Matricheta, and afterward the 150 hymns of the same poet. When they are able to recite these, they begin the study of the Sutras of their sacred canon. They also learn by heart the *Jatakamala*, which gives an account of Buddha in former states of existence. Speaking of what he calls the islands of the Southern Sea, which he visited after leaving India, I-tsing says: 'There are more than ten islands in the South Sea. There both priests and laymen recite the *Jatakamala*, as they recite the hymns mentioned before; but it has not yet been translated into Chinese.'

One of these stories, he proceeds to say, was versified by a king and set to music, and was performed before the public with a band and dancing—evidently a Buddhist mystery play.

I-tsing then gives a short account of the system of education. Children, he says, learn the forty-nine letters and the 10,000 compound letters when they are six years old, and generally finish them in half a year. This corresponds to about 300 verses, each *sloka* of thirty-two syllables. It was originally taught by Mahesvara. At eight years, children begin to learn the grammar of Panini, and know it after about eight months. It consists of 1,000 *slokas*, called Sutras.

Then follows the list of roots and the three appendices, consisting again of 1,000 *slokas*. Boys begin the three appendices when they are ten years old, and finish them in three years.

When they have reached the age of fifteen, they begin to study a commentary on the grammar (Sutra) and spend five years in learning it. And here I-tsing gives the following advice to his countrymen, many of whom came to India to learn Sanskrit, but seem to have learnt it imperfectly. 'If men of China,' he writes, 'go to India, wishing to study there, they should first of all learn these grammatical works, and then only other subjects; if not, they will merely waste their labour. These works should be learnt by heart. But this is suited for men of high quality only.... They should study hard day and night, without letting a moment pass for idle repose. They should be like Confucius, through whose hard study the binding of his *Yih-king* was three times cut asunder, being worn away; and like Sui-shih, who used to read a book repeatedly one hundred times.' Then follows a remark, more intelligible in Chinese than in English: The hairs of a bull are counted by thousands, the horn of a unicorn is only one.'

I-tsing then speaks of the high degree of perfection to which the memory of these students attained, both among Buddhists and heretics. 'Such men,' he says, 'could commit to memory the contents of two volumes, learning them only once.'

And then turning to the *heretics*, or what we should call the orthodox Brahmans, he says: 'The Brahmans are regarded throughout the five divisions of India as the most respectable. They do not walk with the other three castes, and other mixed classes of people are still further dissociated from them. They revere their Scriptures, the four Vedas, containing about 100,000 verses.... The Vedas are handed down from mouth to mouth, not written on paper. There are in every generation some intelligent Brahmans who can recite those 100,000 verses.... I myself saw such men.'

Here then we have an eye-witness who, in the seventh century after Christ, visited India, learnt Sanskrit, and spent about twenty years in different monasteries—a man who had no theories of his own about oral tradition, but who, on the contrary, as coming from China, was quite familiar with the idea of a written, nay, of a printed literature: and yet what does he say? 'The Vedas are not written on paper, but handed down from mouth to mouth.'

Now, I do not quite agree here with I-tsing. At all events, we must not conclude from what he says that there existed no Sanskrit MSS at all at his time. We know they existed. We know that in the first century of our era Sanskrit MSS were carried from India to China and translated there. Most likely therefore there were MSS of the Veda also in existence. But I-tsing, for all that, was right in supposing that these MSS were not allowed to be used by students, and that they had always to learn the Veda by heart and from the mouth of a properly qualified teacher. The very fact that in the later law-books severe punishments are threatened against persons who copy the Veda or learn it from a MS, shows that MSS existed, and that their existence interfered seriously with the ancient privileges of the Brahmans, as the only legitimate teachers of their sacred scriptures.

If now, after having heard this account of I-tsing, we go back for about another thousand years, we shall feel less sceptical in accepting the evidence which we find in the so-called Pratisakhyas, that is, collections of rules which, so far as we know at present, go back to the fifth century before our era, and which tell us almost exactly the same as what we can see in India at the present moment namely that the education of children of the three twice-born castes, the Brahmanas, Kshatriyas, and Vaisyas, consisted in their passing at least eight years in the house of a *guru*, and learning by heart the ancient Vedic hymns.

The art of teaching had even at that early time been reduced to a perfect system, and at that time certainly there is not the slightest trace of anything, such as a book, or skin, or parchment, a sheet of paper, pen or ink, being known even by name to the people of India; while every expression connected with what we should call literature, points to a literature (we cannot help using that word) existing in memory only, and being handed down with the most scrupulous care by means of oral tradition.

I had to enter into these details because I know that, with our ideas of literature, it requires an effort to imagine the bare possibility of a large amount of poetry, and still more of prose, existing in any but a written form. And yet here too we only see what we see elsewhere, namely that man, before the great discoveries of civilization were made, was able by greater individual efforts to achieve what to us, accustomed to easier contrivances, seems almost impossible. So-called savages were able to chip flints, to get fire by rubbing sticks of wood, which baffles our handiest workmen. Are we to suppose that, if they wished to preserve some songs which, as they believed, had once secured them the favour of their gods, had brought rain from heaven, or led them on to victory, they would have found no means of doing so? We have only to read such accounts as, for instance, Mr. William Wyatt Gill has given us in his *Historical Sketches of Savage Life in Polynesia*, to see how anxious even savages are to preserve the records of their ancient heroes, kings, and gods, particularly when the dignity or nobility of certain families depends on these songs, or when they contain what might be called the title-deeds to large estates. And that the Vedic Indians were not the only savages of antiquity who discovered the means of preserving a large literature by means of oral tradition, we may learn from Caesar, not a very credulous witness, who tells us that the 'Druids were said to know a large number of verses by heart; that some of them spent twenty years in learning them, and that they considered it wrong to commit them to writing'—exactly the same story which we hear in India.

We must return once more to the question of dates. We have traced the existence of the Veda, as handed down by oral tradition, from our days to the days of I-tsing in the seventh century after Christ, and again to the period of the Pratisakhyas, in the fifth century before Christ.

In that fifth century BC took place the rise of Buddhism, a religion built up on the ruins of the Vedic religion, and founded, so to say, on the denial of the divine authority ascribed to the Veda by all orthodox Brahmans.

Whatever exists therefore of Vedic literature must be accommodated within the centuries preceding the rise of Buddhism, and if I tell you that there are three periods of Vedic literature to be accommodated, the third presupposing the second, and the second the first, and that even that first period presents us with a collection, and a systematic collection of Vedic hymns, I think you will agree with me that it is from no desire for an extreme antiquity, but simply from a respect for facts, that students of the Veda have come to the conclustion that these hymns, of which the MSS do not carry us back beyond the fifteenth century after Christ, took their origin in the fifteenth century before Christ.

One fact I must mention once more, because I think it may carry conviction even against the stoutest scepticism.

I mentioned that the earliest inscriptions discovered in India belong to the reign of King Asoka, the grandson of Chandragupta, who reigned from 274-237 before Christ. What is the language of those inscriptions? Is it the Sanskrit of the Vedic hymns? Certainly not. Is it the later Sanskrit of the Brahmanas and Sutras? Certainly not. These inscriptions are written in the local dialects as then spoken in India, and these local dialects differ from the grammatical Sanskrit about as much as Italian does from Latin.

What follows from this? First, that the archaic Sanskrit of the Veda had ceased to be spoken before the third century BC. Secondly, that even the later literary and grammatical Sanskrit was no longer spoken and understood by the people at large; that Sanskrit therefore had ceased, nay, we may say, had long ceased to be the spoken language of the country when Buddhism arose, and that therefore the youth and manhood of the ancient Vedic language lie far beyond the period that gave birth to the teaching of Buddha, who, though he may have known Sanskrit, and even Vedic Sanskrit, insisted again and again on the duty that his disciples should preach his doctrines in the language of the people whom they wished to benefit.

And now, when the time allotted to me is nearly at an end, I find, as it always happens, that I have not been able to say one half of what I hoped to say as to the lessons to be learnt by us in India, even with regard to this one branch of human knowledge only, the study of the origin of religion. I hope, however, I may have succeeded in showing you the entirely new aspect which the old problem of the *theogony*, or the origin and growth of the Devas or gods, assumes from the light thrown upon it by the Veda. Instead of positive theories, we now have positive facts, such as you look for in vain anywhere else; and though there is still a considerable interval between the Devas of the Veda, even in their highest form and such concepts as Zeus, Apollon, and Athene, yet the chief riddle is solved, and we know now at last what stuff the gods of the ancient world were made of.

But this theogonic process is but one side of the ancient Vedic religion, and there are two other sides of at least the same importance and of even a deeper interest to us.

There are in fact three religions in the Veda, or, if I may say so, three naves in one great temple, reared as it were, before our eyes by poets, prophets, and philosophers. Here, too, we can watch the work and the workmen. We have not to deal with hard formulas only, with unintelligible ceremonies, or petrified fetishes. We can see how the human mind arrives by a perfectly rational process at all its later irrationalities. This is what distinguishes the Veda from all other sacred books. Much, no doubt, in the Veda also, and in the Vedic ceremonial, is already old and unintelligible, hard and petrified. But in many cases the development of names and concepts, their transition from the natural to the supernatural, from the individual to the general, is still going on, and it is for that very reason that we find it so difficult, nay almost impossible, to translate the growing thoughts of the Veda into the full-grown and more than full-grown language of our time.

Let us take one of the oldest words for god in the Veda, such as deva, the Latin *deus*. The dictionaries tell you that *Deva* means god and gods, and so, no doubt, it does. But if we always translated *Deva* in the Vedic hymns by god, we should not be translating, but completely transforming the thoughts of the Vedic poets. I do not mean only that *our* idea of God is totally different from the idea that was intended to be expressed by *Deva*; but even the Greek and Roman concept of gods would be totally inadequate to convey the thoughts imbedded in the Vedic *Deva*. *Deva* meant originally bright, and nothing else. Meaning bright, it was constantly used of the sky, the stars, the sun, the dawn, the day, the spring, the rivers, the earth; and when a poet wished to speak of all of these by one and the same word—by what we should call a general term—he called them all Devas. When that had been done, Deva did no longer mean 'the Bright ones,' but the name comprehended all the qualities which the sky and the sun and the dawn shared in common, excluding only those that were peculiar to each.

Here you see how, by the simplest process, the Devas, the bright ones, might become and did become the Devas, the heavenly, the kind, the powerful, the invisible, the immortal—and, in the end, something very like the *Theoi* of Greeks and the *Dii* of the Romans.

In this way one Beyond, the Beyond of Nature, was built up in the ancient religion of the Veda, and peopled with Devas, and Asuras, and Vasus, and Adityas, all names for the bright solar, celestial, diurnal, and vernal powers of nature, without altogether excluding, however, even the dark and unfriendly powers, those of the night, of the dark clouds, or of winter, capable of mischief, but always destined in the end to succumb to the valour and strength of their bright antagonists.

We now come to the second nave of the Vedic temple, the second Beyond that was dimly perceived and grasped and named by the ancient *rishis*, namely the world of the Departed Spirits.

There was in India, as elsewhere, another very early faith, springing up naturally in the hearts of the people, that their fathers and mothers, when they departed this life, departed to a Beyond, wherever it might be, either in the East from whence all the bright Devas seemed to come, or more commonly in the West, the land to which they seemed to go, called in the Veda the realm of Yama or the setting sun. The idea that beings which once had been, could ever cease to be, had not yet entered their minds; and from the belief that their fathers existed somewhere, though they could see them no more, there arose the belief in another Beyond, and the germs of another religion.

Nor was the actual power of fathers quite imperceptible or extinct even after their death. Their presence continued to be felt in the ancient laws and customs of the family, most of which rested on their will and their authority. While their fathers were alive and strong, their will was law; and when, after their death, doubts or disputes arose on points of law or custom, it was but natural that the memory and the authority of the fathers should be appealed to settle such points—that the law should still be their will.

Thus Manu says: 'On the path on which his fathers and grandfathers have walked, on that path of good men let him walk, and he will not go wrong.'

In the same manner then in which, out of the bright powers of nature, the Devas or gods had arisen, there arose out of predicates shared in common by the departed, such as Pitris, Fathers, Preta, gone away, another general concept, what we should call *Manes,* the kind ones, *Ancestors, Shades, Spirits* or *Ghosts,* whose worship was nowhere more fully developed than in India. That common name, *Pitris* or Fathers gradually attracted towards itself all that the fathers shared in common. It came to mean not only fathers, but invisible, kind, powerful, immortal, heavenly beings, and we can watch in the Veda, better perhaps than anywhere else, the inevitable, yet most touching metamorphosis of ancient thought,—the love of the child for father and mother becoming transfigured into an instinctive belief in the immortality of the soul.

It is strange, and really more than strange, that not only should this important and prominent side of the ancient religion of the Hindus have been ignored; but that of late its very existence should have been doubted. I feel obliged, therefore, to add a few words in support of what I have said just now of the supreme importance of this belief in and this worship of ancestral spirits in India from the most ancient to the most modern times. Mr. Herbert Spencer, who has done so much in calling attention to ancestor-worship as a natural ingredient of religion among all savage nations, declares in the most emphatic manner, 'that he has seen it implied, that he has heard it in conversation, and that he now has it before him in print, that no Indo-European or Semitic nation, so far as we know, seems to have made a religion of the worship of the dead.' I do not doubt his words, but I think that no so important a point, Mr. Herbert Spencer ought to have named his authorities. It seems to me almost impossible that anybody who has ever opened a book on India should have made such a statement. There are hymns in the *Rigveda* addressed to the Fathers. There are full descriptions of the worship due to the Fathers in the Brahmanas and Sutras. The epic poems, the law books, the Puranas, all are brimful of allusions to ancestral offerings. The whole social fabric of India, with its laws of inheritance and marriage, rests on a belief in the Manes,—and yet we are told that no Indo-European nation seems to have made a religion of the worship of the dead.

The Persians had their *Fravashis,* the Greeks their *theoi patrooi* and their *daimones,*while among the Romans the *Lares familiares* and the *Divi Manes* were worshipped more zealously than any other gods. Manu goes so far as to tell us in one place: 'An oblation by Brahmans to their ancestors transcends an oblation to the deities;' and yet we are told that no Indo-European nation seems to have made a religion of the worship of the dead.

Such things ought really not to be, if there is to be any progress in historical research, and I cannot help thinking that what Mr. Herbert Spencer meant was probably no more than that some scholars did not admit that the worship of the dead formed the whole of the religion of any of the Indo-European nations. That, no doubt, is perfectly true, but it would be equally true, I believe, of almost any other religion. And on this point again the students of anthropology will learn more, I believe, from the Veda than from any other book.

In the Veda the Pitris, or fathers, are invoked together with the Devas, or gods, but they are not confounded with them. The Devas never become Pitris, and though such adjectives as Deva are sometimes applied to the Pitris, and they are raised to the rank of the older classes of Devas, it is easy to see that the Pitris, and Devas had each their independent origin, and that they represent two totally distinct phases of the human mind in the creation of its objects of worship. This is a lesson which ought never to be forgotten.

We read in the *Rigveda*: 'May the rising Dawns protect me, may the flowing Rivers protect me, may the firm Mountains protect me, may the Fathers protect me at this invocation of the gods.' Here nothing can be clearer than the separate existence of the Fathers, apart from the Dawns, the Rivers, and the Mountains, though they are included in one common invocation of the gods.

We must distinguish, however, from the very first, between two classes, or rather between two concepts of Fathers, the one comprising the distant, half-forgotten, and almost mythical ancestors of certain families or of what would have been to the poets of the Veda, the whole human race, the other consisting of the Fathers who had but lately departed, and who were still, as it were, personally remembered and revered.

The old ancestors in general approach more nearly to the gods. They are often represented as having gone to the abode of Yama, the ruler of the departed, and to live there in company with some of the Devas.

Yama himself is sometimes invoked as if he were one of the Fathers, the first of mortals that died or that trod the path of the Fathers leading to the common sunset in the West. Still his real Deva-like nature is never completely lost, and, as the god of the setting sun, he is indeed the leader of the Fathers, but not one of the Fathers himself.

Many of the benefits which men enjoyed on earth were referred to the Fathers, as having first been procured and first enjoyed by them. They performed the first sacrifices, and secured the benefits arising from them. Even the great events in nature, such as the rising of the sun, the light of the day and the darkness of the night, were sometimes referred to them, and they were praised for having broken open the dark stable of the morning and having brought out the cows, that is, the days. They were even praised for having adorned the night with stars, while in later writings the stars are said to be the lights of the good people who have entered into heaven. Similar ideas, we know, prevailed among the ancient Persians, Greeks, and Romans. The Fathers are called in the Veda truthful (*satya*), wise (*suvidatra*), righteous (*ritavat*), poets (*kavi*), leaders (*pathikrit*), and one of their most frequent epithets is *somya*, delighting in Soma, Soma being the ancient intoxicating beverage of the Vedic *rishis*, which was believed to bestow immortality, but which had been lost, or at all events had become difficult to obtain by the Aryas, after their migration into the Punjab.

The families of the Bhrigus, the Angiras, the Atharvans all have their Pitris or Fathers, who are invoked to sit down on the grass and to accept the offerings placed there for them. Even the name of Pitriyajna, sacrifice of the Fathers, occurs already in the hymns of the *Rigveda*.

The following is one of the hymns of the *Rigveda* by which those ancient Fathers were invited to come to their sacrifice:

1. 'May the Soma-loving Fathers, the lowest, the highest, and the middle, arise. May the gentle and righteous Fathers who have come to life (again), product us in these invocations!

2. 'May this salutation be for the Fathers today, for those who have departed before or after; whether they now dwell in the sky above the earth, or among the blessed people.

3. 'I invited the wise Fathers . . . may they come hither quickly, and sitting on the grass readily partake of the poured-out draught!

4. 'Come hither to us with your help, you Fathers who sit on the grass! We have prepared these libations for you, accept them! Come hither with your most blessed protection, and give us health and wealth without fail!

5. 'The Soma-loving Fathers have been called hither to their dear viands which are placed on the grass. Let them approach, let them listen, let them bless, let them protect us!

6. 'Bending your knee and sitting on my right, accept all this sacrifice. Do not hurt us, O Fathers, for any wrong that, we may have committed against you, men as we are.

7. 'When you sit down on the lap of the red dawns, grant wealth to the generous mortal! O Fathers, give of your treasure to the sons of this man here, and bestow vigour here on us!

8. 'May Yama, as a friend with friends, consume the offerings according to his wish, united with those old Soma-loving Fathers of ours, the Vasishthas, who arranged the Soma draught.

9. 'Come hither, O Agni, with those wise and truthful Fathers who like to sit down near the hearth, who thirsted when yearning for the gods, who knew the sacrifice, and who were strong in praise with their songs.

10.'Come, O Agni, with those ancient fathers who like to sit down near the hearth, who for ever praise the gods, the truthful, who eat and drink our oblations, making company with Indra and the gods.

11. 'O Fathers, you who have been consumed by Agni, come here, sit down on your seats, you kind guides! Eat of the offering which we have placed on the turf, and then grant us wealth and strong offspring!

12.'O Agni, O Jatavedas, at our request thou hast carried the offerings, having first rendered them sweet. Thou gavest them to the Fathers and they fed on their share. Eat also, O god, the proffered oblations!

13. 'The Fathers who are here, and the Fathers who are not here, those whom we know, and those whom we know not, thou, Jatavedas, knowest how many they are, accept the well-made sacrifice with the sacrificial portions!

14. 'To those who, whether burnt by fire or not burnt by fire, rejoice in their share in the midst of heaven, grant thou, O King, that their body may take that life which they wish for!'

Distinct from the worship offered to these primitive ancestors, is the reverence which from an early time was felt to be due by children to their departed father, soon also to their grandfather, and great-grandfather. The ceremonies in which these more personal feelings found expression were of a more domestic character, and allowed therefore of greater local variety.

It would be quite impossible to give here even an abstract only of the minute regulations which have been preserved to us in the Brahmanas, the Srauta, Grihya, and Samayacharika Sutras, the Law-books, and a mass of later manuals on the performance of endless rites, all intended to honour the departed. Such are the minute prescriptions as to times and seasons, as to altars and offerings, as to the number and shape of the sacrificial vessels, as to the proper postures of the sacrificers, and the different arrangements of the vessels, that it is extremely difficult to catch hold of what we really care for, namely, the thoughts and intentions of those who first devised all these intricacies. Much has been written on this class of sacrifices by European scholars also, beginning with Colebrooke's excellent essays on 'The Religious Ceremonies of the Hindus,' first published in 1798. But when we ask the simple question. What was the thought from whence all this outward ceremonial sprang, and what was the natural craving of the human heart which it seemed to satisfy, we hardly get an intelligible answer anywhere. It is true that Sraddhas continue to be performed all over India to the present day, but we know how widely the modern ceremonial has diverged from the rules laid down in the old Sastras, and it is quite clear from the descriptions given to us by recent travellers that no one can understand the purport even of these survivals of the old ceremonial, unless he understands Sanskrit and can read the old Sutras. We are indeed told in full detail how the cakes were made which the Spirits were supposed to eat, how many stalks of grass were to be used on which they had to be offered, how long each stalk ought to be, and in what direction it should be held. All the things which teach us nothing are explained to us in abundance, but the few things which the true scholar really cares for are passed over, as if they had no interest to us at all, and have to be discovered under heaps of rubbish.

In order to gain a little light, I think we ought to distinguish between:

1. The daily ancestral sacrifice, the Pitriyajna, as one of the five Great Sacrifices (Mahayajnas);

2. The monthly ancestral sacrifice, the Pindapitriyajna, as part of the New and Full-Moon sacrifice;

3. The funeral ceremonies on the death of a householder;

4. The Agapes, or feasts of love and charity, commonly called Sraddhas, at which food and other charitable gifts were bestowed on deserving persons in memory of the deceased ancestors. The name of Sraddha belongs properly to this last class only, but it has been transferred to the second and third class of sacrifices also, because Sraddha formed an important part in them.

The daily Pitriyajna or Ancestor-worship is one of the five sacrifices, sometimes called the Great Sacrifices, which every married man ought to perform day by day. They are mentioned in the *Grihyasutras*, as Devayajna, for the Devas, Bhutayajna, for animals etc., Pitriyajna, for the Fathers, Brahmayajna, for Brahman, i.e., study of the Veda, and Manushyayajna, for men, i.e., hospitality, etc., Manu (III.70) tells us the same.

The performance of this daily Pitriyajna seems to have been extremely simple. The householder had to put his sacred cord on the right shoulder, to say 'Svadha to this Fathers,' and to throw the remains of certain offerings towards the South.

The human impulse to this sacrifice, if sacrifice it can be called, is clear enough. The five 'great sacrifices' comprehended in early times the whole duty of man from day to day. They were connected with his daily meal. When this meal was preparing, and before he could touch it himself, he was to offer something to the Gods, a Vaisvadeva offering, in which the chief deities were Agni, Soma, the Visve Devas, Dhanvantari, a kind of Aesculapius, Kuhu and Anumati (phase of the moon), Prajapati, lord of creatures, Dyava-prithivi, Heaven and Earth, and Svishtakrit, the fire on the hearth.

After having thus satisfied the Gods in the four quarters, the householder had to throw some oblations into the open air, which were intended for animals, and in some cases for invisible beings, ghosts, and such like. Then he was to remember the departed, the

Pitris, with some offerings; but even after having done this he was not yet to begin his own repast, unless he had also given something to strangers (*atithis*).

When all this had been fulfilled, and when, besides, the householder, as we should say, had said his daily prayers, or repeated what he had learnt of the Veda, then and then only was he in harmony with the world that surrounded him, the five Great Sacrifices had been performed by him, and he was free from all the sins arising from a thoughtless and selfish life.

This Pitriyajna, as one of the five daily sacrifices, is described in the Brahmanas, the Grihya and Samayacharika Sutras,and,of course,in the legal Samhitas. Rajendralal Mitra informs us that 'orthodox Brahmans to this day profess to observe all these five ceremonies, but that in reality only the offerings to the gods and manes are strictly observed, while the reading is completed by the repetition of the Gayatri only, and charity and feeding of animals are Usual and uncertain.'

Quite different from this simple daily ancestral offering is the Pitriyajna or Pindapitriyajna,, which forms part of many of the statutable sacrifices, and, first of all, of the New Moon sacrifice. Here again the human motive is intelligible enough. It was the contemplation of the regular course of nature, the discovery of order in the coming and going of the heavenly bodies, the growing confidence in some ruling power of the world which lifted man's thoughts from his daily work to higher regions, and filled his heart with a desire to approach these higher powers with praise, thanksgiving, and offerings. And it was at such moments as the waning of the moon that his thoughts would most naturally turn to those whose life had waned, whose bright faces were no longer visible on earth, his fathers or ancestors. Therefore at the very beginning of the New-Moon sacrifice, we are told in the Brahmanas and in the Srautasutras, that a Pitriyajna, a sacrifice to the Fathers, has to be performed. A Caru or pie had to be prepared in the Dakshinagni, the southern fire, and the offerings, consisting of water and round cakes (*pindas*), were specially dedicated to father, grandfather, and great-grandfather, while the wife of the sacrificer, if she wishes for a son, was allowed to eat one of the cakes.

Similar ancestral offerings took place during other sacrifices too, of which the New and Full-Moon sacrifices form the general type.

It may be quite true that these two kinds of ancestral sacrifices have the same object and share the same name, but their character is different; and if, as has often been the case, they are mixed up together, we lose the most important lessons which a study of the ancient ceremonial should teach us. I cannot describe the difference between these two Pitriyajnas more decisively than by pointing out that the former was performed by the father of a family, or, if we may say so, by a layman, the latter by a regular priest, or a class of priests, selected by the sacrificer to act in his behalf. As the Hindus themselves would put it, the former is a *grihya*, a domestic, the latter a *srauta*, a priestly ceremony.

We now come to a third case of ceremonies which are likewise domestic and personal, but which differ from the two preceding ceremonies by their occasional character, I mean the funeral, as distinct from the ancestral ceremonies. In one respect these funeral ceremonies may represent an earlier phase of worship than the daily and monthly ancestral sacrifices. They lead up to them, and, as it were, prepare the departed for their future dignity as Pitris or Ancestors. On the other hand, the conception of Ancestors in general must have existed before any departed person could have been raised to that rank, and I therefore preferred to describe the ancestral sacrifices first.

Nor need I enter here very fully into the character of the special funeral ceremonies of India. Their spirit is the same as that of funeral ceremonies of Greeks, Romans, Slavonic, and Teutonic nations, and the coincidences between them all are often most surprising.

In Vedic times the people in India both burnt and buried their dead, and they did this with a certain solemnity, and, after a time, according to fixed rules. Their ideas about the status of the departed, after their body had been burnt and their ashes buried, varied considerably, but in the main they seem to have believed in a life to come, not very different from our life on earth, and in the power of the departed to confer blessings on their descendants. It soon therefore became the interest of the survivors to secure the favour of their departed friends by observances and offerings which, at first, were the spontaneous manifestation of human feelings, but which soon became traditional, technical, in fact, ritual.

On the day on which the corpse had been burnt, the relatives bathed and poured out a handful of water to the deceased, pronouncing his name and that of his family. At sunset they returned home, and, as was but natural, they were told to cook nothing during the first night, and to observe certain rules during the next day up to ten days, according to the character of the deceased. These were days of mourning, or, as they were afterwards called, days of impurity, when the mourners withdrew from contact with the world, and shrank by a natural impulse from the ordinary occupations and pleasures of life.

Then followed the collecting of the ashes on the 11th, 13th or 15th day of the dark half of the moon. On returning from thence they bathed, and then offered what was called a Sraddha to the departed.

This word Sraddha, which meets us here for the first time, is full of interesting lessons, if only properly understood. First of all it should be noted that it is absent, not only from the hymns, but, so far as we know at present, even from the ancient Brahmanas. It seems therefore a word of a more modern origin. There is a passage in Apastamba's *Dharmasutras* which betrays, on the part of the author, a consciousness of the more modern origin of the Sraddhas:

'Formerly men and gods lived together in this world. Then the gods in reward of their sacrifices went to heaven, but men were left behind. Those men who perform sacrifices in the same manner as the gods did, dwelt (after death) with the gods and Brahman in heaven. Now (seeing man left behind) Manu revealed this ceremony which is designated by the word Sraddha.'

Sraddha has assumed many meanings, and Manu, for instance, uses it almost synonymously with Pitriyajna, But its original meaning seems to have been 'that which is given with *sraddha* or faith;' i.e., charity bestowed on deserving persons, and, more particularly, on Brahmanas. The gift was called Sraddha, but the act itself also was called by the same name. The word is best explained by Narayana in his commentary on the *Grihyasutras* of Asvalayana, 'Sraddha is that which is given in faith to Brahmans for the sake of the Fathers.'

Such charitable gifts flowed most naturally and abundantly at the time of a man's death, or whenever his memory was revived by happy or unhappy events in a family, and hence Sraddha has become the general name for ever so many sacred acts commemorative of the departed. We hear of Sraddhas not only at funerals, but at joyous events also, when presents were bestowed in the name of the family, and therefore in the name of the ancestors also, on all who had a right to that distinction.

It is a mistake therefore to look upon Sraddhas simply as offerings of water or cakes to the Fathers. An offering to the Fathers was, no doubt, a symbolic part of each Sraddha, but its more important character was charity bestowed in memory of the Fathers.

This, in time, gave rise to much abuse, like the alms bestowed on the church during the Middle Ages. But in the beginning the motive was excellent. It was simply a wish to benefit others, arising from the conviction, felt more strongly in the presence of death than at any other time, that as we can carry nothing out of this world, we ought to do as much good as possible in the world with our worldly goods. At Sraddhas the Brahmanas were said to represent the sacrificial fire into which the gifts should be thrown. If we translate here Brahmanas by priests, we can easily understand why there should have been in later times so strong a feeling against Sraddhas. But priest is a very bad rendering of Brahmana. The Brahmanas were, socially and intellectually, a class of men of high breeding. They were a recognised and, no doubt, a most essential element in the ancient society of India. As they lived for others, and were excluded from most of the lucrative pursuits of life, it was a social, and it soon became a religious duty, that they should be supported by the community at large. Great care was taken that the recipients of such bounty as was bestowed at Sraddhas should be strangers, neither friends nor enemies, and in no way related to the family. Thus Apastamba says: 'The food eaten (at a Sraddha) by persons related to the giver is a gift offered to goblins. It reaches neither the Manes nor the Gods.' A man who tried to curry favour by bestowing Sraddhika gifts, was called by an opprobrious name, a Sraddhamitra.

Without denying therefore that in later times the system of Sraddhas may have degenerated, I think we can perceive that it sprang from a pure source, and, what for our present purpose is even more important, from an intelligible source.

Let us now return to the passage in the *Grihyasutras* of Asvalayana, where we met for the first time with the name of Sraddha. It was the Sraddha to be given for the sake of the departed, after his ashes had been collected in an urn and buried. This Sraddha is called *ekoddhishta*, or, as we should say, personal. It was meant for one person only, not for the three ancestors, nor for all the ancestors. Its object was in fact to raise the departed to the rank of a Pitri, and this had to be achieved by Sraddha offerings continued during a whole year. This at least is the general, and, most likely, the original rule. Apastamba says that the Sraddha for a deceased relative should be performed every day during the year, and that after that a monthly Sraddha only should be performed or none at all, that is, no more personal Sraddha, because the departed shares henceforth in the regular Parvana-sraddhas.

When the Sraddha is offered on account of an auspicious event, such as birth or a marriage, the fathers invoked are not the father, grandfather, and great-grandfather, who are sometimes called *asura-mukha*, with tearful faces, but the ancestors before them, they are called *nandimukha*, or joyful.

Colebrooke, to whom we owe an excellent description of what a Sraddha is in modern times, took evidently the same view. 'The first set of funeral ceremonies,' he writes, 'is adapted to effect, by means of oblations, the re-embodying of the soul of the deceased, after burning his corpse. The apparent scope of the second set is to raise his shade from this world, where it would else, according to the notions of the Hindus, continue to roam among demons and evil spirits, up to heaven, and then deify him, as it were, among the manes of departed ancestors. For this end, a Sraddha should regularly be offered to the deceased on the day after the mourning expires; twelve other Sraddhas *singly* to the deceased in twelve successive months; similar obsequies at the end of the third fortnight, and also in the sixth month, and in the twelfth; and the oblation called Sapindana on the first anniversary of his decease. At this Sapindana Sraddha, which is the last of the *ekoddistha* Sraddhas, four funeral cakes are offered to the deceased and his three ancestors, that consecrated to the deceased being divided into three portions and mixed with the other three cakes. The portion retained is often offered to the deceased, and the act of union and fellowship becomes complete.'

When this system of Sraddhas had once been started, it seems to have spread very rapidly. We soon hear of the monthly Sraddha, not only in memory of one person lately deceased, but as part of the Pitriyajna, and as obligatory, not only on householders, but on other persons also, and not, only on the three upper castes, but even, without hymns, on Sudras, and as to performed, not only on the day of New Moon, but on other days also, whenever there was an opportunity.

The same difficulties which confront us when we try to form a clear conception of the character of the various ancestral ceremonies, were felt by the Brahmans themselves, as may be seen from the long discussions in the commentary on the Sraddha-kalpa.

We may safely say, therefore, that not a day passed in the life of the ancient people of India on which they were not reminded of their ancestors, both near and distant, and showed their respect for them, partly by symbolic offerings to the Manes, partly by charitable gifts to deserving persons, chiefly Brahmans. These offertories varied from the simplest, such as milk and fruits, to the costliest, such as gold and jewels. The feasts given to those who were invited to officiate or assist at a Sraddha seem in some cases to have been very sumptuous, and what is very important, the eating of meat, which in later times was strictly forbidden in many sects, must, when the Sutras were written, have been fully recognised.

This shows that these Sraddhas, though possibly of later date than the Pitriyajnas, belong nevertheless to a very early phase of Indian life. And though much may have been changed in the outward form of these ancient ancestral sacrifices, their original solemn character has remained unchanged. Even at present, when the worship of the ancient Devas is ridiculed by many who still take part in it, the worship of the ancestors and the offering of Sraddhas have maintained much of their old sacred character. They have sometimes been compared to the 'communion' in the Christian Church, and it is certainly true that many natives speak of their funeral and ancestral ceremonies with a hushed voice and with real reverence. They alone seem still to impart to their life on earth a deeper significance and a higher prospect. I could go even a step further and express my belief, that the absence of such services for the dead and of ancestral commemorations is a real loss in our own religion. Almost every religion recognises them as tokens of a loving memory offered to a father, to a mother, or even to a child, and though in many countries they may have proved a source of superstition, there runs through them all a deep well of living human faith that ought never to be allowed to perish. The early Christian Church had to sanction the ancient prayers for the souls of the departed, and in more southern countries the services on All Saints' and on All Souls'. Day continue to satisfy a craving of the human heart which must be satisfied in every religion. We, in the North, shrink from these open manifestations of grief but our hearts know often a deeper bitterness; nay, there would seem to be a higher truth than we at first imagine in the belief of the ancients that the souls of our beloved ones leave us no rest, unless they are appeased by daily prayers, or, better still, by daily acts of goodness in remembrance of them.

But there is still another Beyond that found expression in the ancient religion of India. Besides the Devas or Gods, and besides the Pitris or Fathers there was a third world, without which the ancient religion of India could not have become what we see it in the Veda. That third Beyond was what the poets of the Veda call the Rita, and which I believe meant originally no more than 'the straight line.' It is applied to the straight line of the sun in its daily course, to the straight line followed by day and night, to the straight line that regulates the seasons, to the straight line which, in spite of many momentary deviations, was discovered to run through the whole realm of nature. We call that Rita, that straight, direct, or right line, when we apply it in a more general sense, the Law of Nature; and when we apply it to the moral world, we try to express the same idea again by speaking of the Moral Law, the law on which our life is founded, the eternal Law of Right and Reason, or, it may be, 'that which makes for righteousness' both within us and without.

And thus, as a thoughtful look on nature led to the first perception of bright gods, and in the end of a God of light, as love of our parents was transfigured into piety and a belief in immortality, a recognition of the straight lines in the world without, and in the world within, was raised into the highest faith, a faith in a law that underlies everything, a law in which we may trust, whatever befall, a law which speaks within us with the divine voice of conscience, and tell us 'this is Rita,' 'this is right,' 'this is true,' whatever the statutes of our ancestors, or even the voices of our bright gods, may say to the contrary.

These three Beyonds are the three revelations of antiquity; and it is due almost entirely to the discovery of the Veda that we, in this nineteenth century of ours, have been allowed to watch again these early phases of thought and religion, which had passed away long before the first beginnings of other literatures. In the Veda an ancient city has been laid bare before our eyes which, in the history of all other religions, is filled up with rubbish, and built over by new architects. Some of the earliest and most instructive scenes of our distant childhood have risen once more above the horizon of our memory which, until thirty or forty years ago, seemed to have vanished for ever.

Only a few words more to indicate at least how this religious growth in India contained at the same time the germs of Indian philosophy. Philosophy in India is, what it ought to be, not the denial, but the fulfilment of religion; it is the highest religion, and the oldest name of the oldest system of philosophy in India is Vedanta, that is, the end, the goal, the highest object of the Veda.

Let us return once more to Yaska, that ancient theologian who lived in the fifth century BC, and who told us that, even before his time, all the gods had been discovered to be but three gods, the gods of the Earth, the gods of the Air, and the gods of the Sky, invoked under various names. The same writer tells us that in reality there is but *one* God, but he does not call him the Lord, or the Highest God, the Creator, Ruler and Preserver of all things, but he calls him *Atman*, the Self. The one *Atman* or Self, he says, is praised in many ways owing to the greatness of the godhead. And he then goes on to say: 'The other gods are but so many members of the one *Atman*, Self, and thus it has been said that the poets compose their praises according to the multiplicity of the natures of the beings whom they praise.'

It is true, no doubt, that this is the language of a philosophical theologian, not of an ancient poet. Yet these philosophical reflections belong to the fifth century before our era, if not to an earlier date; and the first germs of such thoughts may be discovered in some of the Vedic hymns also. I have quoted already from the hymns such passages as—'They speak of Mitra, Varuna, Agni; then he is the heavenly bird Garutmat; *that which is and is one* the poets all in various ways: they speak of Yama, Agni, Atarisvan.'

In another hymn, in which the sun is likened to bird, we read:Wise poets represent by their words the bird who is one, in many ways.'

All this is still tinged with mythology; but there are other passages from which a purer light beams upon us, as when one poet asks:

'Who saw him when he was first born, when he who has no bones bore him who has bones? Where was the breath, the blood, the Self of the world? Who went to ask this from any that knew it?'

Here, too, the expression is still helpless, but though the flesh is weak, the spirit is very willing. The expression 'He who has bones' is meant for that which has assumed consistency and form, the Visible, as opposed to that which has no bones, no body, no form, the Invisible, while 'breath, blood, and self of the world' are but so many attempts at finding names and concepts for what is by necessity inconceivable, and therefore unnameable.

In the second period of Vedic literature, in the so-called Brahmanas, and more particularly in what is called the Upanishads, or the

Vedanta portion, these thoughts advance to perfect clearness and definiteness. Here the development of religious thought, which took its beginning in the hymns, attains to its fulfilment. The circle becomes complete. Instead of comprehending the One by many names, the many names are now comprehended to be the One. The old names are openly discarded; even such titles as Prajapati, lord of creatures, Visvakarman, maker of all things, Dhatri, creator, are put aside as inadequate. The name now used is an expression of nothing but the purest and highest subjectiveness,—it is *Atman*, the Self, far more abstract than our Ego,—the Self of all things, the Self of all the old mythological gods—for they were not *mere* names, but names intended for something—lastly, it is the Self in which each individual self must find rest, must come to himself, must find his own true Self.

You may remember that I spoke to you in my second lecture of a boy who insisted on being sacrificed by his father, and who, when he came to Yama, the ruler of the departed, was granted three boons, and who then requested, as his third boon, that Yama should tell him what became of man after death. That dialogue forms part of one of the Upanishads, it belongs to the Vedanta, the end of the Veda, the highest aim of the Veda. I shall read you a few extracts from it.

Yama, the King of the Departed, says:

'Men who are fools, dwelling in ignorance, though wise in their own sight, and puffed up with vain knowledge, go round and round, staggering to and fro, like blind led by the blind.

'The future never rises before the eyes of the careless child, deluded by the delusions of wealth. *This* is the world, he thinks; there is no other; thus he falls again and again under my sway (the sway of death).

'The wise; who by means of meditating on his *Self*, recognises the Old (the old man within) who is difficult to see, who has entered into darkness, who is hidden in the cave, who dwells in the abyss, as God, he indeed leaves joy and sorrow far behind.

'That Self, the Knower, is not born, it dies not; it came from nothing, it never became anything. The Old man is unborn, from everlasting to everlasting; he is not killed, though the body be killed.

'That Self is smaller than small, greater than great; hidden in the heart of the creature. A man who has no more desires and no more griefs, sees the majesty of the Self by the grace of the creator.

'Though sitting still, he walks far; though lying down, he goes everywhere. Who save myself is able to know that God, who rejoices, and rejoices not?

'That Self cannot be gained by the Veda; nor by the understanding, nor by much learning. He whom the Self chooses, by him alone the Self can be gained. The Self chooses him as his own.

'But he who has not first turned away from his wickedness, who is not calm and subdued, or whose mind is not at rest, he can never obtain the Self, even by knowledge.

'No mortal lives by the breath that goes up and by the breath that goes down. We live by another, in whom both repose.

'Well then, I shall tell thee this mystery, the eternal word (Brahman), and what happens to the *Self*, after reaching death.

Some are born again, as living beings, others enter into stocks and stones, according to their work, and according to their knowledge.

'But he, the Highest Person, who wakes in us while we are asleep, shaping one lovely sight after another, he indeed is called the Light,' he is called Brahman, he alone is called the Immortal. All worlds are founded on it, and no one goes beyond. *This is that.*

'As the one fire, after it has entered the world, though one, becomes different according to what it burns, thus the One Self within all things, becomes different, according to whatever it enters, but it exists also apart.

'As the sun, the eye of the world, is not contaminated by the external impurities seen by the eye, thus the One Self within all things is never contaminated by the sufferings of the world, being himself apart.

'There is one eternal thinker, thinking non-eternal thoughts; he, though one, fulfils the desires of many. The wise who perceive Him within their Self, to them belongs eternal life, eternal peace.

'Whatever there is, the whole world, when gone forth (from Brahman), trembles in his breath. That Brahman is a great terror, like a drawn sword. Those who know it, become immortal.

'He (Brahman) cannot be reached by speech, by mind, or by the eye. He cannot be apprehended, except by him who says, *He is.*

'When all desires that dwell in the heart cease, then the mortal becomes immortal, and obtains Brahman.

'When all the fetters of the heart here on earth are broken, when all that binds us to this life is undone, then the mortal becomes immortal—here my teaching ends.'

This is what is called Vedanta, the Veda-end, the end of the Veda, and this is the religion or the philosophy, whichever you like to call it, that has lived on from about 500 BC to the present day. If the people of India can be said to have now any system of religion at all,—apart from their ancestral sacrifices and their Sraddhas, and apart from mere caste-observances,—it is to be found in the Vedanta philosophy, the leading tenets of which are known to some extent in every village. That great revival of religion, which was inaugurated some fifty years ago by Ram Mohun Roy, and is now known as the Brahma Samaj, under the leadership of my noble friend Keshub Chunder Sen, was chiefly founded on the Upanishads, and was Vedantic in spirit. There is, in fact, an unbroken continuity between the most modern and the most ancient phases of Hindu thought, extending over more than three thousand years.

To the present day India acknowledges no higher authority in matters of religion, ceremonial, customs, and law than the Veda, and so long as India is India, nothing will extinguish that ancient spirit of Vedantism which is breathed by every Hindu from his earliest youth, and pervades in various forms the prayers even of the idolater, the speculations of the philosopher, and the proverbs of the beggar.

For purely practical reasons therefore,—I mean for the very practical object of knowing something of the secret springs which determine the character, the thoughts and deeds, of the lowest as well as of the highest amongst the people in India,—an acquaintance with their religion, which is founded on the Veda, and with their philosophy, which is founded on the Vedanta is highly desirable.

It is easy to make light of this, and to ask, as some statesmen have asked, even in Europe, what has religion, or what has philosophy, to do with politics? In India, in spite of all appearances to the contrary, and notwithstanding the indifference on religious matters so often paraded before the world by the Indians themselves, religion, and philosophy too, are great powers still. Read the account that has lately been published of two native statesmen, the administrators of two first-class states in Saurashtra, Junagadh and Bhavnagar, Gokulaji and Gaurisankara, and you will see whether the Vedanta is still a moral and a political power in India or not.

But I claim even more for the Vedanta, and I recommend its study, not only to the candidates for the Indian Civil Service, but to all true students of philosophy. It will bring before them a view of life, different from all other views of life which are placed before us in the history of philosophy. You saw how behind all the Devas or gods, the authors of the Upanishads discovered the *Atman* or Self. Of that Self they predicated three things only, that it is, that it perceives, and that it enjoys eternal bliss. All other predicates were negative: it is not this, it is not that—it is beyond anything that we can conceive or name.

But that Self, that Highest Self, the *Paramatman*, could be discovered after a severe moral and intellectual discipline only, and those who had not yet discovered it, were allowed to worship lower gods, and to employ more poetical names to satisfy their human wants. Those who knew the other gods to be but names or persons—*personae* or masks, in the true sense of the word—knew also that those who worshipped these names or persons, worshipped in truth the Highest Self, though ignorantly. This is a most characteristic feature in the religious history of India. Even in the *Bhagavadgita*, a rather popular and exoteric exposition of Vedantic doctrines, the Supreme Lord or Bhagavat himself is introduced as saying: 'Even those who worship idols, worship me.'

But that was not all. As behind the names of Agni, Indra, and Prajapati, and behind all the mythology of nature, the ancient sages of India had discovered the *Atman*—let us call it the objective Self—they perceived also behind the veil of the body, behind the senses, behind the mind, and behind our reason (in fact behind the mythology of the soul, which we often call psychology), another *Atman*, or the subjective Self. That Self, too, was to be discovered by a severe moral and intellectual discipline only, and those who wished to find it, who wished to know, not themselves, but their Self, had to cut far deeper than the senses, or the mind, or the reason, or the ordinary Ego. All these too were mere Devas, bright apparitions—mere names—yet names meant for something. Much that was most dear, that had seemed for a time their very self, had to be surrendered, before they could find the Self of Selves, the Old Man, the Looker-on, a subject independent of all personality, an existence independent of all life.

When that point had been reached, then the highest knowledge began to dawn, the Self within (the *Pratyagatman*) was drawn towards the Highest Self (the *Paramatman*), it found its true self in the Highest Self, and the oneness of the subjective with the objective Self was recognised as underlying all reality, as the dim dream of religion,—as the pure light of philosophy.

This fundamental idea is worked out with systematic completeness in the Vedanta philosophy, and no one who can appreciate the lessons contained in Berkeley's philosophy, will read the Upanishads and the *Brahmasutras* and their commentaries without feeling a richer and a wiser man.

I admit that it requires patience, discrimination, and a certain amount of self-denial before we can discover the grains of solid gold in the dark mines of Eastern philosophy. It is far easier and far more amusing for shallow critics to point out what is absurd and rediculous in religion and philosophy of the ancient world than for the earnest student to discover truth and wisdom under strange disguises. Some progress, however, has been made, even during the short span of life that we can remember. *The Sacred Books of the East* are no longer a mere butt for the invectives of missionaries or the sarcasms of philosophers. They have at last been recognised as historical documents, aye, as the most ancient documents in the history of the human mind, and as palaeontological records of an evolution that begins to elicit wider and deeper sympathies than the nebular formation of the planet on which we dwell for a season, or the organic development of that chrysalis which we call man.

If you think that I exaggerate, let me read you in conclusion what one of the greatest philosophical critics—and certainly not a man given to admiring the thoughts of others—says of the Vedanta, and more particularly of the Upanishads. Schopenhauer writes:

'In the whole world there is no study so beneficial and so elevating as that of the Upanishads. It has been the solace of my life—it will be the solace of my death.'

I have thus tried, so far as it was possible in one course of lectures, to give you some idea of ancient India, of its ancient literature, and, more particularly, of its ancient religion. My object was, not merely to place names and facts before you, these you can find in many published books, but, if possible, to make you see and feel the general human interests that are involved in that ancient chapter of the history of the human race. I wished that the Veda and its religion and philosophy should not only seem to you curious or strange, but that you should feel that there was in them something that concerns ourselves, something of our own intellectual growth, some recollections, as it were, of our own childhood, or at least of the childhood of our own race. I feel convinced that, placed as we are here in this life, we have lessons to learn from the Veda, quite as important as the lessons we learn at school from Homer and Virgil, and lessons from the Vedanta quite as instructive as the systems of Plato or Spinoza.

I do not mean to say that everybody who wishes to know how the human race came to be what it is, how language came to be what it is, how religion came to be what it is, how manners, customs, laws and forms of government came to be what they are, how we ourselves came to be what we are, must learn Sanskrit, and must study Vedic Sanskrit. But I *do* believe that not to know what a study of Sanskrit, and particularly a study of the Veda, has already done for illuminating the darkest passages in the history of the human mind, of that mind on which we ourselves are feeding and living, is a misfortune, or, at all events, a loss, just as I should count it a loss to have passed through life without knowing something, however little, of the earth and its geological formation, of the movements of the sun, the moon, and the stars,—and of the thought, or the will, or the law, that governs these movements.

NOTES

Pages

127. **Ionians:** One of the three great branches of the Greek race, Dorians and Achaeans being the others.

128. **Milletus:** A rich Greek city on the Aegean coast of Asia Minor.

Herodotus: 484-425 BC Greek historian born at Halicarnassus. His *Histories* are very attractive and contain much information based on his personal observation and on hearsay on the peoples of antiquity and their legends.

Anaximander (610-547 BC): Ionian philosopher, friend and disciple of Thales, the founder of the Ionian school.

Anaximenes (of Miletus): Another philosopher of the same school; died about 480 BC. He is believed to have perfected the sun-dial.

129. **Aeschylos** (525-456 BC): The father of Greek tragedy; one of the world's greatest poets and thinkers.

Peisistratos and Polycrates: Tyrants in the Greek sense of the word) of Athens and Samos respectively.

Seleucus: General of Alexander the Great; succeeded to his Asiatic possessions at the break up of his empire, and founded the line of Seleucidae who ruled in Syria (312-64 BC).

Aramacan: A generic name for Semitic tribes who inhabited Aram, a swampy region near the mouths of the Euphrates and the Tigris.

dextrorsum: going from left to right.

sinistrorsum: going from right to left.

130. **Srotriya:** from *Srotra* meaning 'ear' ; *sruti* (lit. hearing) means the Veda.

132. **Tamralipti:** Now Tamluk in the Midnapore district, near the mouth of the Hugli river.

Nalanda: In Bihar; the great Buddhist monastery (also a university) of this place has been partly excavated in recent years and this has added much to the knowledge of the later history of Buddhism (Mahayana).

Jatakamala: Garland of birth-stories, by Aryasura, a Buddhist writer of perhaps the fifth century AD.

Islands of the Southern Sea: The Malay Archipelago.

sloka: verse; here a unit of reckoning, 32 letters.

133. **Confucius**: The most celebrated Chinese philosopher and founder of an ethical religion marked by conspicuous good sense and love of humanity. His whole system rests on the reciprocal duties of men—between princes and subjects, parents and children, and among fellow citizens.
Yih-king: One of the most ancient sacred books of the Chinese.
Sui-shih: An early Chinese teacher.
134. **Pratisakhyas:** Manuals of phonetics for the use of particular Vedic schools; *prati*—'each', *sakha*—'branch', 'school'.
138. **Herbert Spencer** (1820-1903): English philosopher and sociologist.
139. **Fravashis:** Benevolent ancestor-spirits.
142. **Srauta, Grihya and Samayacharika Sutras:** Manuals dealing respectively with sacrificial ritual, domestic ritual, and social conduct. Each 'school' had its own set of these manuals.
the law-books: Written in verse like Manu, Yajnavalkya, and others.
Sraddha: A ceremony in honour and for the benefit of dead relatives observed with great strictness at various fixed periods and on occasions of rejoicing as well as mourning by the surviving relatives—(Monier-Williams).
Sastras: Authoritative manuals of sacred law or knowledge.
143. **Svadha:** means 'own portion or share'—(Monier-Williams).
Aesculapius: Greek god of medicine.
144. **legal samhitas:** Compilations of later times.
Rajendralal Mitra: (1824-91): Bengali scholar and antiquarian; President of the Asiatic Society of Bengal.
146. **Apastamba:** A renowned sage and writer on ritual of the *Black Yajurveda*. His sutras have survived in their entirety (thirty sections).
Asvalayana: The founder of one of the schools of the *Rigveda*.
154. **Gokulaji**: As a young man Gokulaji, the son of a good family, learnt Persian and Sanskrit. His chief interest in life, in the midst of a most successful political career, was the 'Vedanta'. A little insight, we are told, into this knowledge turned his heart to higher objects, promising him freedom from grief, and blessedness, the highest aim of all. This was the turning point of his inner life. When the celebrated Vedanti anchorite, Rama Bava, visited Junagadh, Gokulaji became his pupil. When another anchorite, Paramahansa Sachchidananda, passed through Junagadh on a pilgrimage to Girnar, Gokulaji was regularly initiated in the secrets of the Vedanta. He soon became highly proficient in it, and through the whole course of his life, whether in power or in disgrace, his belief in the doctrines of the Vedanta supported him, and made him, in the opinion of English statesmen, the model of what a native statesman ought to be—(M.M.).
Gaurisankara (Udayasankar, 1805-91): Entered the service of Bhavnagar in 1822 and rose to the position of Diwan in 1846. After a long and successful administration, he retired in 1879. He became C.S.I. in 1877. He turned an ascetic (Sannyasi) in 1886.
155. **Berkeley** (George, 1684-1753): Irish philosopher, a rigorous Idealist, who held that to be real is to be perceived.
Brahmasutras: of Badarayana; uncertain date, but doubtless not much later than the beginning of the Christian era. The work has been commented on by philosophers of many schools, each interpreting its aphorisms in his own sense. The commentaries of Ṣankara, Ramanuja, Srikantha, and Madhva are among the best known.

156. **Sacred Books of the East:** A series of 51 volumes of translations of oriental religious books, planned and edited by Max Müller with the co-operation of many scholars.

Schopenhauer (Aurther, 1788-1860): German philosopher; a brilliant writer.

Spinoza (1632-77): Monistic philosopher who held mind and matter to be attributes of one infinite substance, finite existences being modes thereof.

Topics for Essays

1. Ideals of Research.
2. The place of lectures and examination in modern education.
3. The Aryan race and culture.
4. Religion as a social force.
5. The role of the village in India.
6. The value of Sanskrit learning.
7. Climate and culture.
8. Hindu view of Life.
9. The historical value of the *Rigveda*.
10. Foreign influence in Vedic culture.
11. Poetry in primitive religion.
12. Physical Religion.
13. 'No name is a mere name'.
14. The influence of writing on the growth of literature.
15. Origin and significance of ancestor-worship.

Index